Theology of Peace

Theology of Peace

Paul Tillich

Edited and introduced by
Ronald H. Stone

Westminster/John Knox Press
Louisville, Kentucky

© 1990 Westminster/John Knox Press

All rights reserved—no part of this book may be reproduced in any form without permission in writing from the publisher, except by a reviewer who wishes to quote brief passages in connection with a review in magazine or newspaper.

Cover photo by Rolf Pelikan

Book design by Gene Harris

First edition

For Acknowledgments, see page 7.

Published by Westminster/John Knox Press
Louisville, Kentucky

PRINTED IN THE UNITED STATES OF AMERICA
9 8 7 6 5 4 3 2 1

Library of Congress Cataloging-in-Publication Data

Tillich, Paul, 1886–1965.
   Theology of peace / by Paul Tillich ; edited and introduced by Ronald H. Stone. — 1st ed.
        p.   cm.
   Includes bibliographical references.
   ISBN 0-664-25118-8

   1. Peace—Religious aspects—Christianity. 2. Christianity and international affairs. 3. Christianity and politics.
4. Christianity and justice. 5. World politics—20th century.
I. Stone, Ronald H. II. Title.
BT736.4.T55   1990
261.8′73—dc20   90-32387

Contents

Acknowledgments

The theme of Paul Tillich on peace has been of interest to me since my earlier work, *Paul Tillich's Radical Social Thought* (Atlanta: John Knox Press, 1980; reprinted, Lanham, Md.: University Press of America, 1986). A trip to the Paul Tillich Archive at the Andover-Harvard Theological Library in Cambridge, Massachusetts, in the spring of 1989 was financed by a Travel Collections Program grant from the National Endowment for the Humanities. My deepest expression of thanks is extended to Dr. Mutie Tillich Farris for her help and for granting the permission of the Paul Tillich Estate for the publication of this work.

Grateful acknowledgment is made for permission to reprint the following material:

"The Kingdom of God and History," by H. G. Wood et al. Copyright 1938 by Willett, Clark and Company. Reprinted by permission of Harper & Row, Publishers, Inc. Published in Great Britain by George Allen & Unwin, London, 1938. Reproduced by kind permission of Unwin Hyman Ltd.

"Spiritual Problems of Postwar Reconstruction," reprinted with permission from *Christianity & Crisis*, vol. 2, no. 14 (1942). Copyright 1942, Christianity & Crisis, 537 West 121st Street, New York, NY 10027.

"A Program for a Democratic Germany," reprinted with permission from *Christianity & Crisis*, vol. 4, no. 8 (1944). Copyright 1944, Christianity & Crisis, 537 West 121st Street, New York, NY 10027.

"The World Situation," reprinted with permission of Charles Scribner's Sons, an imprint of Macmillan Publishing Company, from Henry P. Van Dusen, ed., *The Christian Answer.* Copyright 1945 Charles Scribner's Sons; copyright renewed © 1973 Henry P. Van Dusen. Reprinted with permission of Derek Van Dusen. Subheadings are reprinted from this essay as published in *The World Situation* (Fortress Press, 1965), edited by Franklin Sherman. Used by permission of Augsburg Fortress.

"The Hydrogen Bomb," *Pulpit Digest,* vol. 34, no. 194 (June 1954). Used by permission of Harper & Row, Publishers, Inc.

"Boundaries," translated by Franklin Littell, reprinted by permission from *The Journal of Bible and Religion*, vol. 33, no. 1 (1965). Reprinted by permission of the Börsenverein des Deutschen Buchhandels, Frankfurt am Main, and Walter de Gruyter & Co., Berlin. The title and key words have been changed from "Frontiers" to "Boundaries" by permission of the publishers.

"On 'Peace on Earth,' " an essay published in *To Live as Men: An Anatomy of Peace,* 1965. Reprinted by permission of the Center for the Study of Democratic Institutions.

"The Right to Hope," reprinted from *Neue Zeitschrift für systematische Theologie und Religionsphilosophie,* vol. 7 (1965), by permission of Walter de Gruyter & Co., Berlin.

Introduction

We have Christian peace movements. To serve them we need a theology hopeful enough to inspire them and rigorous enough to sustain them for the long struggle. The thought of Paul Tillich is adequate to the task. He called his social thought "faithful realism," and he thereby refused to ignore the realities of the brokenness of the world or the reality of the world's divine purposes. Beneath the existential horror of world politics, glimpses of divine essence are discernible, and theological analysis can bring them into clearer focus.

This volume is a gift to the peace movements. It suggests ways to focus peace work for all of humanity's seeking for peace. The analysis is Christian and theological, but the work is done in a way that makes its insights available to all who seek peace. Tillich's work has suggestions both for the church and for humanity in its ecumenical breadth. In fact, the deepening of ecumenical dialogue among faith communities is one of Tillich's passionately held convictions about the work for religious peacemakers.

Theology of Peace is composed of twelve essays. They were written from 1938 to 1965 and represent major efforts of Tillich to think theologically about peace, from the eve of the Second World War to the crisis of Berlin and nuclear armaments in the mid-1960s. The work is of long-lasting value to peace thinking. Many specific references reflect the times and conflicts in which the essays were written. Tillich's existential and political commitments required particular stands in his day. The reader will need to move through specific times and politically bound judgments to apply the theology to our own time.

At first glance, Paul Tillich seems an unlikely source for a theology of peace. Europe had two major wars in the twentieth century, and he participated in both. As a chaplain in the First World War, he endured trenches awash with the blood and bodies of the western front;[1] he received a medal from the German empire and then fell from nervous exhaustion. The war and the defeat of Germany destroyed his bourgeois, idealistic life and cast him into a revolutionary social existence. In the Second World War, he participated as an agent of Allied propaganda, broadcasting regularly on religious, philosophical, and political topics to Germany over the Voice of America.[2] He gave his talents to articulating war aims and organizing German refugees against the Nazi regime.

Readers of only the *Systematic Theology* will find little comfort from his few words on peace. Earthly fulfillment of peace is not expected.

> The Kingdom of God fulfills the utopian expectation of a realm of peace and justice while liberating them from their utopian character by the addition "of God," for with this addition the impossibility of an earthly fulfillment is implicitly acknowledged.[3]

Yet the Kingdom of God is immanent as well as transcendent. One expression of the immanence of the Kingdom of God was its fighting in history to defeat Hitler's Germany.[4]

Within the *Systematic Theology* both churches and nations must find their way between the antinomies of pacifism or militarism and of cynical realism or utopian idealism. In a brief paragraph Tillich suggests that the way through seems to lie in considerations of "just

[1]"Sermons" in the Paul Tillich Archive, Andover-Harvard Theological Library, Cambridge, Massachusetts.
[2]Paul Tillich, *An meine deutschen Freunde* (Stuttgart: Evangelisches Verlagswerk, 1973).
[3]*Systematic Theology*, vol. 3 (Chicago: University of Chicago Press, 1963), p. 358.
[4]Ibid., p. 387.

war," but that judgment is of existential risk and subject to "incertitude."[5] There is, however, an absolute judgment:

> The churches as representatives of the Kingdom of God can and must condemn a war which has only the appearance of a war but is in reality universal suicide. One never can start an atomic war with the claim that it is a just war, because it cannot serve the unity which belongs to the Kingdom of God. But one must be ready to answer in kind, even with atomic weapons, if the other side uses them first. The threat itself could be a deterrent.[6]

This paragraph clearly indicates his own position, a position which differed from that of his country and NATO. It is a deterrent posture but also a policy of no just first use. Following this judgment he returns to the question of church policy and recognizes the appropriateness and even necessity for the church to honor pacifism as a symbolic representation of the Kingdom of God. The churches, however, must refrain from imposing pacifist demands on political leadership.

Peace for Tillich remained a religious hope. Plans that people of goodwill could impose a peace on a dynamic world remained a utopian illusion. Speaking in postwar Germany, he said:

> In America this conception is widely held. It finds expressions among other places in the English version of the angels' anthem at the birth of Christ. The biblical text reads, "good will to men," which is rendered, "to men of good will." This conception is one of the most fantastic utopias I have ever encountered. Ever again and again, one meets this belief that sooner or later many men of good will—and naturally we include ourselves among them—will obtain permanent control of things and then peace on earth will be realized.[7]

---

[5]Ibid.
[6]Ibid., pp. 387–388.
[7]Paul Tillich, *Political Expectation*, ed. James Luther Adams (New York: Harper & Row, 1971), p. 140.

His polemic against both soft utopians and hard
utopians would carry him into critique of the peace
work of both John Foster Dulles and Pope John XXIII.
It remains a constant of his peace writing. To move into
his theory of peace, his shorter, more occasional writings are collected here.[8]

1. "The Kingdom of God and History"

Paul Tillich's fight against National Socialism in the
halls of his university, in newspapers, in his manifesto
against the Third Reich, and in his published political
philosophy resulted in his exile in 1933. From his new
home in New York and his teaching posts at Union
Theological Seminary and Columbia University, he returned to Europe in 1936 to try to organize intellectu-
als against National Socialism, and he engaged in
polemical debate with German theologians who supported Adolf Hitler, including a former friend. In 1937
at the Oxford Conference on Life and Work he delivered the major paper published here. The National
Socialist government of Germany denied German theologians the visas necessary for participation in the
meeting.

This paper is essential to understanding Tillich's theology of peace, for here the Kingdom of God as the
meaning of history is explicated. The central concepts
of kairos and the demonic are explained in the effort to
read the "signs of the times" in the tumultuous events
of prewar European history. Our present-day Christian
peace movements have come to accept the doctrine of
the kairos, but they are still confused over the relevance of the concept of "the demonic." In the 1930s
the social breakdown of economic suffering and the
cyclical breakdown of unregulated capitalism, the passions of violent nationalism, and the tyranny of Bolshevism were regarded as the bearers of the demonic.
Forces that contained value had become distorted and

---

[8]The bibliographical details of these essays are in *Register, Bibliographie
und Textgeschichte zu den Gesammelten Werke von Paul Tillich* (Stuttgart:
Evangelisches Verlagswerk, 1975). *Gesammelte Werke,* vol. 14.

were threatening humanity. World peace remained a goal, but pacifism and moralism were inadequate to achieve it. World peace would require the overthrow of nationalism and the unification of humanity. That was impossible under conditions of tyranny or social insecurity. Contemporary American readers may want to read his commitments to religious socialism as a faith-filled fight for the struggle of the poor and unemployed for social participation, security, and dignity. Such a reading is a good translation of his nonpartisan meaning of religious socialism. The paper was published first in *The Kingdom of God and History* (1938), which also included chapters by H. G. Wood, C. H. Dodd, Edwyn Bevan, Eugene Lyman, H. D. Wendland, and Christopher Dawson. The original publisher was George Allen & Unwin of London.

2. "The Meaning of Anti-Semitism"

The relationship among Jews, Germans, and Christians was a central problem for Tillich. A few days before Hitler came to power, Tillich had stressed the Jewish contribution to German culture in the Founder's Day address at the University of Frankfurt. His defense of Jewish students and his critique of Third Reich policies toward Jews were directly involved in his dismissal from the university. So it was no surprise that when breaking political silence in his new homeland his first address was on anti-Semitism. The address was given to a full house at a protest meeting in Madison Square Garden on November 21, 1938. He called for Christians, German Americans, Jews, and others to unite against the demonry expressed in National Socialism's anti-Semitism. His call for "an uncompromising no" to Germany's rulers echoed his 1937 call for church "resistance" to nationalism. It was published in *Radical Religion*, vol. 4, no. 1 (1938), and in *German People's Echo*, vol. 2, no. 48 (1938).

3. "Spiritual Problems of Postwar Reconstruction"

Literature and art had testified to the breakdown of the human spirit in nineteenth- and twentieth-century Europe. Mass society, bureaucracy, and mechanization eroded the human factors of spirituality as expressed in both personality and community. The war, Tillich wrote in 1942, was of a world in revolution, but victory in war would not restore the human spirit. The failure of personality and community was rooted in the failure to grasp meaningful lives. Victory could not restore the creative, dynamic part of the human soul. The victors could, however, protect rather than crush dynamic centers of meaning trying to be reborn in Europe. Tillich's plea was that, in the approaching victory, governments would permit autonomous groups seeking the ultimate meaning of life to develop and to contribute to the rediscovery of personality and community. The essay with its warnings about American society probes the depths of modern meaninglessness. The text is reprinted here from *Christianity and Crisis,* vol. 2, no. 14 (August 10, 1942).

4. "Christian Basis of a Just and Durable Peace"

Three lectures from 1943 demonstrate the interconnectedness of Tillich's Protestant theology, the question of social welfare of modern humanity, and the necessity for overcoming the balance of power politics of the nation-state system.

John Foster Dulles, Secretary of State, 1953–1959, whose temperament and policies seem so far removed from Paul Tillich, had many associations with him. Dulles was on the Board of Directors of Union Theological Seminary (1945–1953) during Tillich's tenure. Dulles's father had been a professor at Auburn Seminary, which joined Union in New York City, and his daughter and son were graduates of theological seminaries. Both Dulles and Tillich were associated in the work of the Oxford Conference on Life and Work of 1937. In 1943, the Federal Council of Churches' Commission on a Just and Durable Peace asked Tillich to make a theological contribution to its work. John Foster Dulles was the chairperson and driving force of the commission's work. Tillich chose in three lectures to attack the philosophical basis of the commission's work, which he perceived as overly legalistic and utopian—characteristic aspects of John Foster Dulles's work in foreign policy. Though the lectures were critical of the commission's assumptions, the differences should not be exaggerated. The commission was very effective in rallying church support for the concept and development of the United Nations, a goal close to Tillich's thought about world peace.

John Foster Dulles's philosophical mentor Henri Bergson had learned some of his philosophy of life from Friedrich Schelling, whose thought Tillich had absorbed, and the commission's work had some of the early Dulles's philosophy of change and world development in it. It lacked Tillich's sense of a world in revolt against the capitalist spirit. Dulles evolved into a hardened proponent of the capitalist spirit against Marxism, in contrast to Tillich's direction. These later differences are present in embryo in Tillich's critique of his host's thought, but the sharp divergences became even more evident after the war.

The commission included leading American Protestant thinkers about foreign policy, among them Walter van Kirk and John C. Bennett. In its efforts for the United Nations, the commission became one of the most effective examples of liberal Protestant thought shaping United States foreign policy.

The first lecture, "Christian Principles and Political Reality," explored the depths of Tillich's theological thinking. It related love, power, and justice to life as the dynamic actuality of being. The dynamics of life pushing for change in the foundation of the world situation made the preservation of any status quo impossible. Justice as the form of the unifying power of being was in contradiction to "the durable." The world was in revolt against the world economic situation, and the durable could not be just.

The second lecture, "The Social Problem of a Just and Durable Peace," focused on a world in revolution. Tillich's analysis described a revolt against the chaos of a world subjected to the Leviathan of monopoly capitalism. Economic insecurity produced meaninglessness and resigned adjustment to heteronomous powers that stifled the human spirit. The way to go was represented by British socialist movements, central European underground movements, democratic socialists in Germany, and New Deal trends in the United States, in alliance with possible liberalizing tendencies in Russia. Liberal planning for planned state economies was needed. Without gains for the individual to participate meaningfully in the process of production, the war sacrifices would be as much in vain as those of the previous world war.

The third lecture, on "The International Problem of a Just and Durable Peace," moved from the social-economic problem to the problem of international relations. Here the movement toward the development of world history could be seen. Yet the emerging reality of world history was destructive. By this time he could not hope for postwar world unity, though he believed regional groupings of nations were still possible. Anglo-Saxon domination of the world was a third possibility. Returning to national sovereignty made no sense. The ecumenical movement of the churches was a positive contribution toward the emergence of a world order. But it was a "not yet." It was as it had been: an "underground center of the world historical process." In conclusion he rejected as arrogant the concept of a just and durable peace and suggested instead concepts of grace and tragedy.

The lectures are in Tillich's handwriting in the Paul Tillich Archive, Andover-Harvard Theological Library, and are here presented for the first time after considerable editing.

5. "Power and Justice in the Postwar World"

Paul Tillich's pessimism about the postwar situation deepened as his hopes for an Allied victory came closer to realization. The essay on power and justice in the postwar world relates Tillich's three central social principles of love, power, and justice. Written and delivered as a speech between June and September 1944 (as indicated by the reference to the invasion of France without any reference to the breakthrough into Germany in September of that year), the essay applies these principles quite specifically to the possibilities of a postwar settlement that Tillich could envisage in 1944.

The introduction to the essay reveals Tillich's own way of working in social philosophy, which was to learn of social trends from other scholars in discussion groups and then relate what he regarded as a reliable reading of the "signs of the times" to his own ontology. At this point in 1944 he was pessimistic about European economic union, which he regarded as necessary for social security in Europe. As Europe approaches economic union today, at least in the West, there are grounds for remembering Tillich's earlier hopes for economic unification of Europe. His fears of a Europe divided between East and West were of course realized, but even that division now appears to be weakening, and ideas of a common European homeland from the Atlantic to the Urals are rising once again.

The essay, previously unpublished, is a typewritten manuscript of nineteen pages from the Paul Tillich Archive, Andover-Harvard Theological Library.

6. "A Program for a Democratic Germany"

In 1944, Paul Tillich formed a group of German exiles to work for the democratization of postwar Germany. The program of the group was partially a group project, but Tillich drafted the original proposal and solicited members to join the Council for a Democratic Germany. The original correspondence of the council and some of the German responses to Tillich's proposal are in the Paul Tillich Archive, Andover-Harvard Theological Library. The program as published represents Paul Tillich's peace plan for Germany, including his warnings against the division of Germany. "A Program for a Democratic Germany" was published in *Christianity and Crisis*, vol. 4, no. 8 (1944), with both German and American signatories.

7. "The World Situation"

The boldest of Paul Tillich's writings on the spiritual-economic-political situation of the world preceded the atomic bomb. In the closing months of World War II he attempted to apply his philosophical thought to the emergence of one world united by war. He analyzed the problem of a world at war to suggest Christian answers to the desperate world situation. The role of the churches in the ecumenical movement, which represented a drive toward world unity, is stressed most strongly in this writing. Christian answers are to be found in both practice and theory, and they can be neither escapist nor utopian. The strengths of humanistic modern culture must be affirmed and its weaknesses negated.

The essay was first published in *The Christian Answer*, edited by Henry P. Van Dusen (New York: Charles Scribner's Sons, 1945). It was republished in 1965 by Fortress Press (Philadelphia), edited by Franklin Sherman, who added the subheadings reprinted here.

8. "The Hydrogen Bomb"

After the war, Tillich served on the Federal Council of Churches commission that published *The Christian Conscience and Weapons of Mass Destruction*. This work stressed that the overriding issue before it was the avoidance of global war without surrender to tyranny. The satanic temptation of preventive war was to be rejected as beyond the limits of tolerable policy. The commission treated war as tragic, but it was not sanguine about agreements to limit weapons development in 1950. The primary agenda had to be work on the moral and political level to overcome the issues of the cold war.

The commission reluctantly sanctioned the position

of deterrence, but warned against any first use of nuclear weapons or any attack that would drive the superpowers to the use of nuclear weapons. The commission, including Tillich, argued that if atomic weapons were used against the United States or its allies, "We believe that it could be justifiable for our government to use them with all possible restraint to prevent the triumph of an aggressor." The report noted that even if individuals would "rather be destroyed than to destroy in such measure," such policies ought not to be urged upon the government, which was responsible for the security and defense of all the people.[9]

In his own writing, Tillich argued that a war fought with nuclear weapons could not be justified. It was not permissible to enter a war that included the intention to use nuclear weapons. Such a war would only bring mutual destruction, and no intended goal of the war could be fulfilled. He noted that Western allies could, if they had the will, develop conventional armaments adequate to deter any Communist invasion in Europe. He leaned toward a position of no first use of nuclear weapons, as the commission had declared, but he also allowed the West some ambiguity in announcing such a policy. Until adequate conventional forces were created, "maybe it was safer to keep the Communists uncertain about first use." However, the logic of deterrence meant that

> our intention to answer any nuclear attack with nuclear weapons must be absolutely clear, and it must also be clear that we have the power to do so.[10]

The correspondence in the Paul Tillich Archive indicates that Tillich was repeatedly requested by the American Friends Service Committee, the National Committee for a Sane Nuclear Policy, and other organizations to endorse their positions against weapons testing and for nuclear disarmament. He refused to give any of these organizations wholehearted support, and

---

[9]*The Christian Conscience and Weapons of Mass Destruction* (New York: Federal Council of the Churches of Christ in America, 1950), p. 14.
[10]Paul Tillich, "Correspondence," *Partisan Review* 39/1 (1962): 311, 312.

he resisted especially their pacifist leanings. He did sign
a statement of the Committee for a Sane Nuclear Policy
(SANE) in 1957 calling for arms control and the abolition of nuclear testing. The statement was published in
The New York Times on November 15, 1957. Other
signers included long-standing pacifists, antiwar acti-
vists, religious leaders, Eleanor Roosevelt, and John
Bennett, whose guidance Tillich sought on these questions. Reinhold Niebuhr, who was a little more of a cold
warrior than John Bennett, refrained from signing,
though on most issues Bennett, Niebuhr, and Tillich
were agreed.

Tillich's Harvard secretary, Grace Leonard, was a
member of SANE, and through her influence Tillich
agreed to SANE's 1961 use of a statement he had published in *Pulpit Digest* in June of 1954 on the dangers
of the hydrogen bomb. That statement (reprinted here)
summarizes his general philosophical position on the
threat of nuclear weapons and argues for the necessity
of resistance to the possibility of nuclear warfare on the
part of everyone who is aware of the situation.

9. "The Ethical Problem of the Berlin Situation"

Tillich's caution about the threatening of the use of
nuclear weapons brought him under the criticism of
James Reston (*The New York Times,* October 25, 1961).
Tillich had appeared on a panel discussion television
program of Eleanor Roosevelt's that included Dean
Rusk, Henry Kissinger, James Reston, and Max Freed-
man. Obviously the panel was dominated by hard-line
cold warriors. Tillich's Christian ethics and central
European origins freed him from the cold war hysteria
over his home city of Berlin and allowed him to discuss
the issue prudently and realistically. Others were more
anxious to defend Berlin with nuclear weapons. Particularly noteworthy in Tillich's analysis, a theme that appeared elsewhere in his writing during this period, is
the insight that even retreat is not the end. Retreat is
a normal strategic move. He knew and wrote in *Partisan Review* in 1962 that in the long run the West was
militarily superior to the Warsaw Pact nations. The

avoidance of retreat was no excuse for relying on nuclear weapons in a suicidal manner. The memorandum reprinted here is the one referred to by James Reston; it is from the Paul Tillich Archive, Andover-Harvard Theological Library.

10. "Boundaries"

On receiving the Peace Prize of the Marketing Association of the German Book Trade in Frankfurt in 1962, Tillich spoke autobiographically and politically about boundaries. Peace emerges as peoples fulfill their mission within the boundaries given to them in history. Conflicts are present, but they do not need to erupt destructively. Boundaries must be seen as permeable and also as limiting. Germany's future is in accepting its finitude, but penetrating the border to the East, and in reducing the division between East and West while contributing to an emerging world civilization. Out of his own experience, Germany's experience, and his central ontological ideas, he weaves a philosophy of peace, power, striving, life, and limits around the concept of boundary. The thought of this German from the East seems particularly relevant to the pressing issues of German reunification. Boundaries are beginning to dissolve, creating dangers and possibilities. The text was published in Germany and also in the United States in *The Journal of Bible and Religion,* vol. 33, no. 1 (1965).

11. "On 'Peace on Earth' "

On February 18, 1965, Tillich delivered a short paper entitled "On 'Peace on Earth' " at a convocation of the Center for the Study of Democratic Institutions occasioned by Pope John XXIII's 1963 encyclical *Pacem in Terris.* Cold warriors had previously been critical of Tillich's rejection of the use of nuclear weapons to defend Berlin.[11] James Reston and Dean Rusk had re-

---

[11]Wilhelm and Marion Pauck, *Paul Tillich* (New York: Harper & Row, 1976), p. 257.

garded his position as unrealistic. Here in this essay, one of his last on politics, his faithful realism is evident.

He praised the Pope's action in issuing the statement, and its emphasis on "the ultimate principle of justice." However, most of his essay was a critique of the encyclical, followed by his own statement of hope for the struggle toward peace. He found the encyclical too much limited to the Western world; this search for peace would have to be more open to traditions other than Western Christian humanism. The encyclical obscured the injustice that would result from resistance to injustice. Power was not sufficiently dealt with in the encyclical; the discussion stayed at an unrealistic level and did not enter into the necessary ambiguities of power. The encyclical also obscured the degree to which moral expectations for groups were different from those of individuals. Finally, the appeal should not have been addressed moralistically to "all men of good will" but to all people, for evil and good are mixed in all humanity.

The encyclical was too close to utopianism for Tillich. Hope—realistic hope—had to be grounded in realities. Tillich could see hope for peace in the fear of mutual destruction, the technical unity of humanity in space conquest, the increasing worldwide dialogue on many fronts, the development of some world legal structures, and a few signs of emerging consensus or communal eros.[12]

He did not hope for a final stage of peace on earth within history. He did hope for fragmentary victory over structures of evil, of which war was one of the greatest. Too-easy speeches for peace created cynicism. The struggle for peace had to be continued even when signs of probable failure were prevalent. He argued that, with a hope for victory, people could work for peace in particular situations even though they knew total peace would elude them. Rejecting utopianism and affirming hope, he urged the conference to begin its work.

The critique of the encyclical is very representative of Tillich's political ethics. The positions of faithful real-

---

[12]Winter, *Social Ethics*, p. 231.

ism, attack on utopianism, emphasis on power, distinction in morals between groups and individuals, and the ambiguity of human existence are all continuous themes in his political writing. Sharing a Christian humanism with the Pope, he draws from his Lutheran heritage a realism that the encyclical lacks, and he looks for hope not so much in moral exhortation but in empirical political realities. The text is reprinted from Gibson Winter, ed., *Social Ethics* (New York: Harper & Row, 1968).

12. "The Right to Hope"

In 1965, the last year of his life, Tillich preached often on hope. The bibliographical information we have (see note 8 above) shows that he preached on the theme of the right to hope in Chicago and San Francisco. The text that concludes this volume is of his sermon of March 28, 1965, at the Memorial Church of Harvard University. It carries forward the themes of the first essay presented here, "The Kingdom of God and History," and indeed of all the essays, inasmuch as peace was a hope. The text is reprinted from *Neue Zeitschrift für systematische Theologie und Religionsphilosophie* (1965).

Paul Tillich had hopes for humanity. They were rooted ontologically in tendencies of what humanity truly is. These tendencies could grow. Yet "world history is a cemetery of broken hopes, of utopias which had no foundation in reality."[13] New tendencies of hope for humanity were in a democratic form of life, in the hopes of the poor for participation, and in movements for human unity.

Certainly enough has been said about the ambiguities of peace. Hopes for peace rest in gains in resolving the terrible problems of poverty and squalor that dominate so much of humanity. They rest in social and political participation in a meaningful democratic life becoming possible for the masses of humanity. They

[13]"The Right to Hope," chapter 12 of this volume.

rest in historical forces pushing for humanity's unity. They rest, as they did in prophetic religion, in seeing that human peace is connected with ecological peace. They find expression in ecumenical spiritual movements reaching reality in Christianity and within other religions. It is to be hoped that new ways of eliminating the anarchy of international relations will accompany the increasing development of world community.

In terms of the immediate policy agenda, I see in Tillich's theology of peace affirmations of priority for policies of no first use of nuclear weapons, actions of individual and corporate resistance to reliance on nuclear terror, work for the social-economic development of the poor world, the trivializing and acceptance of international boundaries, and the increase of ecumenical dialogue and reconciliation.

The peace writings of Paul Tillich have been the subject of some international dialogue. The first major essay on Paul Tillich's peace theology was by Lubomir Mirejovsky, the General Secretary of the Christian Peace Conference. It was published in Czechoslovakia as "Peace Issues in the Work of Paul Tillich" and in the United States in the *Newsletter of the North American Paul Tillich Society,* Robert P. Scharlemann, ed. (14/2 [April 1988]: 5–10).

1

The Kingdom
of God and History

Introduction

The Task

The task with which I have been entrusted is that of giving a religious interpretation of history from the standpoint of the Christian belief in the Kingdom of God. Christian theology, under the influence of Greek thought, has taken almost incredible pains over the problems of the natural and the moral sphere seen in the light of the Christian faith in God. In the sphere of the Christian interpretation of history, however, in spite of some outstanding individual conceptions, the problem of the Kingdom of God and history has received far less attention. This is partly due to the pressure of an ecclesiastical conservatism, which has regarded history as practically consummated in the existence of the church. The opposition of the revolutionary sects, in all the various periods of church history, was not sufficiently strong to break down this barrier. It is only during quite recent years that the question of our historical existence has become central for all vital theological and philosophical thought and discussion. The churches can evade this question only at the cost of a complete withdrawal from the life of the present day. They are summoned to reflect upon the great solutions of their past and to seek for a new solution, expressed in some powerful symbol, which will meet the need of the humanity of the present day in its questionings and its despair.

The Way

The way to this goal leads through a threefold process of reflection. First of all we need a philosophical and theological clarification of the concepts used. It is obvious that this preparatory stage is of more than merely formal significance. Even the most abstract conception of history, and the most formal presentation of the categories which constitute it, includes ultimate philosophical decisions. These, for their part, are dependent on ultimate religious decisions, consequently on religious faith. Thus the preparatory work on the concepts concerned contains, in abstract form, the whole solution.

The second step is the general presentation of the relation between the Kingdom of God and history according to theological principles. Here the task of theology proper outweighs that of philosophy, which is relevant for the first step. Here too, however, it is true that the whole is included in the part. For since theology has to do both with the Logos and with practical life, at least so far as its form and its material are concerned, it is also determined by philosophical and practical decisions.

The third step is the concrete attitude to the historical forces of the present day. Since the only entrance to the interpretation of history is historical action, there is no serious grappling with the problem of history which has not been born out of the necessity for coming to a present historical decision. Philosophical idealism and theological transcendentalism try to conceal this state of affairs. But it comes out clearly in every single interpretation of the historical process, and indeed in every category of interpretation, however abstract it may be. It is therefore more honest and more fruitful to include in the interpretation of history itself the fact that such interpretation is rooted in historical action and, on the other hand, to justify this by means of the actual interpretation.

The Standpoint

The practical standpoint presupposed in the following outline and at the same time to be confirmed by it is that of so-called "religious socialism." It starts with the insight that the bourgeois-capitalistic epoch of occidental development has reached the stage of a most radical transformation which may mean the end of this epoch altogether. Religious socialism links the insight, which is being more and more widely acknowledged by people of historical consciousness, with the special conviction that the coming form of human society must be a socialist one if it is to be adequate to the actual necessities as well as to the moral demands of the situation. The religious interpretation of history explained in this article consequently has two roots—a religious-transcendent root, the Christian message of the Kingdom of God, and a political-immanent root, the socialist interpretation of the present. The former supplies the principles and criteria, the latter the material and the concrete application. This bipolar method is essential for any religious interpretation of history. It does not, however, mean that the theological decisions are subjected to the political ones, neither does it mean that political decision acquires theological dignity. It rather means that the divine claim over the world is not kept within an abstract transcendence but is used for evaluating and molding actual reality. Religious interpretation of history is *"applied theology"* and therefore necessarily bipolar. Any attempt at eliminating the concrete, political pole entails either the destruction of a true interpretation of history or a concealment of the latent political attitude, which in this case becomes effective unconsciously and without criticism. Interpretation of history is subjected to the same methodological demand as the production of a Christian "worldview" or of Christian ethics; there must be the quest for a bipolar beginning.

Part One: Conceptual Preparation

The Concept of History

I

History is the totality of remembered events, which are determined by free human activity and are important for the life of human groups.

History is *remembered* history. Both in German and in English the word "history" has a twofold meaning: subjective and objective. This suggests the fact that history, in the strict sense of the word, begins as soon as historical consciousness arises, which creates historical tradition. But the converse also is true. Historical consciousness and historical tradition arise as soon as history in the strict sense of the word begins. The subjective and the objective element, memory and event, are inseparable.

History is dependent upon free human activity, but it is not dependent on this *alone.* Nature too has a share in the making of human history, insofar as it creates the geographical, biological, and psychological bases for it, and also exercises a constant influence upon human action. But nature itself has no history because it has no freedom. In all nature the existence of things is a necessary result of their essence. In man existence is opposed to his essence. Upon the basis of existence new things happen, which do not follow from essence, but are due to human freedom. Here is the difference between mere becoming and history. (Biological spontaneity may provide a transition from the one to the other, but ultimately it belongs to nature, not to history.)

Among the countless events in which human freedom participates, those alone constitute history which stand in relation to the life of human groups. The action of the individual only gains historical significance through his relation to the life of a social group. This is true even when his action takes the form of *separation* from the social group. Even the hermit in his denial of society is related to society. And only through this relation does the life of the hermit as a whole gain historical significance.

II

Historical groups are all those human groups which on the one hand have the power to exist and to maintain their existence, and on the other hand are the bearers of a definite system of values for the establishment of which the historical group feels responsible. This sense of responsibility is expressed in the form of consciousness of a special vocation.

Every human group may become a "bearer" of history: from the family, by way of the tribe and the nation, perhaps up to a united mankind. Yet mankind as a whole has not hitherto become a "bearer" of history, since it has not achieved a uniform group existence supported by power, nor has it gained a common sense of values.

Historical existence presupposes power, at least the power to exist. Since, however, life only exists while it is growing, the *power of growth* also belongs to historical existence. A group only has the power to exist and to grow in this way if, as a group, it is *united,* that is, when it has the possibility of forming a united political determination. Every living form of power realizes itself in constantly changing discussion with other powers, natural or historical, and out of this the impulse to historical movement is born.

Human freedom implies the consciousness of meaning and value. Accordingly, every historical group feels its existence to be in a special way meaningful and filled with value. No imperialism could develop apart from such a sense of value or of vocation. The nationalism of the Western nations is absolutely bound up with a definite consciousness of vocation.

III

Historical time is directed time—time with an end, a beginning, and a center—and is consequently *qualitative* time, developing in different periods.

Historical time must be distinguished from physical and biological time. In nature the cyclic movement of time predominates; the end returns to the beginning; nothing essentially *new* takes place. In history directed time breaks through the cyclic movement. Something new takes place and replaces the process of mere repetition. Emergent evolution in the biological realm may be considered as a limited anticipation of the historical newness, limited first by the lack of freedom of decision, second by the fact that with the creation of "historical man" biological evolution seems to have reached its summit and end.

From this it follows that history is not merely a continually flowing stream which can be measured by quantitative standards, but that every historical period has a special quality whose character is dependent upon its significance for the total historical process. Thus for the Christian consciousness the time before and after Christ does not only differ quantitatively but qualitatively. The understanding of the total direction of history is decided by the event in which a human group perceives the meaning of its history. We call it the *center* of history. The character of this center then determines the conception of the *aim* of history, and the center is at the same time decisive for the fixing of the beginning of history, that is, that point in time in which a human group for the first time becomes conscious of its historical character. Thus, for instance, from the Christian point of view, *Christ* is the center of history, the realization of his Kingdom is the end, and the first expectation of the Kingdom is the beginning of history.

Historical time cannot be measured in terms of physical time. Billions of years before and after man appeared on the earth neither continue nor frustrate the meaningful direction of history. Neither the end nor the beginning of history can be designated on the plane of physical time.

IV

The meaning of history can be found neither in a final stage of historical development—the ultimate fulfillment of all historical potentialities—nor in an infinite approximation to a fulfillment which can never be reached, nor in a continuous change of historical growth and decay as found in nature, nor in a transcendent supranature unconnected with history.

The idea of a final stage in which history has, so to speak, fulfilled its aim contradicts human nature, since in historical man existence is necessarily contrasted with essence. (This is not a natural necessity, but is made necessary by freedom and fate.) Further, the idea of a final stage would exclude all other stages and all generations of men living in them from the meaning of their historical existence.

The idea of progressive approximation to a final fulfillment can only be applied in three directions. First, in the sense of technical progress, which is the original and adequate meaning of this concept; second, in the sense of a progress in political unification, which is to be considered as a consequence of the technical control of mankind over the whole earth; third, in the sense of the gradual humanization of human relationships. But there is no progress with respect to the creative works of culture or with respect to the morality of mankind. The first is impossible because creativity is a matter of grace, not of growth; the second is impossible because morality is a matter of free decision, and consequently not a matter of delivery and tradition. Education can only communicate the standard and level on which moral decisions can be made, not the decisions themselves. Further, it must be said that an infinite approximation to the final fulfillment would replace the fulfillment by the way toward it; and this is ultimately self-contradictory.

The naturalistic interpretation of history, as for example Spengler's theory of cultural circles which grow up and decay, or the nationalistic interpretation of history from the point of view of national growth and decay, reduces history to the level of nature. In both these

cases the distinction between what is and what ought
to be, between true and false, between good and bad
disappears in favor of self-realization, self-repression,
and power.

History loses its meaning when it is presupposed that
its meaning and value are fulfilled in an eternal world
of essentialities, which is either entirely severed from
historical development or is only accidentally connected with it. Both in the thought of Plato and in that
of Neoplatonism, history is thus emptied of content.
Both interpret the relation between time and eternity
in such a way that what happens in time has no meaning for the eternal at all. Both make nature the pattern
of history either in an idealistic or in a mystical form,
and both miss the significance of history.

V

The ultimate meaning of history is the suprahistorical
unification and purification of all elements of preliminary meaning which have become embodied in historical activities and institutions.

The category of the supranatural is used to express a
closer relationship of the transcendent, ultimate meaning to the immanent, preliminary meaning than the
categories eternal and temporal are able to do. The
suprahistorical is beyond history but it is essentially related to history, while eternity is the mere opposite of
time. It is meaningless to speak of the suprahistorical in
terms of a stage of being, or a form of existence, or
something future which is not yet but will be sometime.
The transcendent cannot be expressed in terms of
being but only in terms of meaning. We understand
what is meant by "unconditioned meaning"—for instance, unconditioned good or truth—but we do not
understand what is meant by "unconditioned being"
because all our thinking is limited to the realm of conditioned beings and its categories.

From this point of view we can affirm only two characteristics of the ultimate meaning of history: it is
unification and purification. Unification means that the
dispersed embodiments of meaning in historical activi-

ties and institutions have an invisible, suprahistorical unity, that they belong to an ultimate meaning of which they are radiations. And purification means that the ambiguous embodiment of meaning in historical realities, social and personal, is related to an ultimate meaning in which the ambiguity, the mixture of meaning and distortion of meaning, is overcome by an unambiguous, pure embodiment of meaning.

Insofar as this unity and purity lie beyond history, we have to state that the meaning of history transcends history. Insofar as nothing is contained in this unity and purity which does not belong to real history and its dispersion and ambiguity, the meaning of history is to be found in history. Both statements are true, but they are true only in connection with each other. In this way historical activity acquires ultimate importance without becoming utopian, and the suprahistorical acquires content without becoming mythological.

The Concept of the Kingdom of God

I

The Kingdom of God is a symbolic expression of the ultimate meaning of existence. The social and political character of this symbol indicates a special relation between the ultimate meaning of existence and the ultimate meaning of human history.

It is a symbolic expression for the relationship of the unconditioned meaning of existence to actual existence. It must be symbolic since it is impossible to grasp this relationship directly and unsymbolically. It is, however, a true symbol, that is, a symbol which irreplaceably stands for what is symbolized. It expresses the majesty, controlling power, and distance of the unconditioned meaning of existence with respect to the realm of conditioned meanings. There are other possible symbols for the same relationship taken from different realms of experience. So, for instance, Paul speaks in a more ontological way of the final stage of existence in which "God will be all in all." In John there are more mystical symbols, such as Eternal Life in

Christ, Friendship with God. All these symbols have in
common the presupposition that being as being is
meaningful, while the doctrine of Nirvana sees the ultimate meaning of existence in the dissolution of being.
"Kingdom" is a symbol taken from the social and
political sphere. It points more than the other symbols
mentioned to the overwhelming importance of human
historical life for the ultimate meaning of existence. It
suggests that human personality, freedom, and community constitute the center of existence, its development
and its fulfillment. Consequently this symbol has to be
the main tool for a Christian interpretation of history.

The historical relation of the symbol "Kingdom of
God" is obvious in the latent contrast implied between
the Kingdom of God and the kingdoms of this world.
The Kingdom of God is expected to triumph over the
kingdoms of this world; it is a dynamic power acting in
history, materializing itself in history although never
becoming identical with history.

II

The contrast between the Kingdom of God and the
kingdoms of this world is expressed most clearly in the
assertion that there is a demonic opposition to the Kingdom of God within the realm of human history. History
in this way becomes a battlefield of the divine and the
demonic.

The "demonic" is a category which was used for the
religious interpretation of history in Persia, in Jewish
apocalypses, in the New Testament, and in the ancient
Christian church up to the time of Augustine. Later this
category emerged again and again in periods of great
historical tension. The loss of it in modern times is connected with the rise of the idea of progress and the
destruction of the original Christian interpretation of
history. It is understandable that the breakdown of the
idea of progress amid the historical catastrophes of the
present and recent past has given a new significance to
this category. Religious socialism was the first to redis-
cover and use it. This was possible only because the
mythological or ontological sense of the demonic, in

which demons are a kind of beings, was sufficiently destroyed, and so the term could be applied to that destructive, blind, chaotic element which is implied in all powerful creating movements and drives them toward final dissolution. While the word "demonic" has this positive and creative connotation, the word "satanic" points to a purely negative principle. The satanic can only be understood as absolute contradiction, while the demonic participates in the divine creative power. Therefore the satanic cannot exist in itself; it needs the positive of which it is contradiction; it has reality only in the reality of the demonic powers which control existence generally, and human existence especially.

When Augustine equates the Kingdom of God with the church and the Kingdom of Satan with the great world empires, he is partly right and partly wrong. He is right in asserting that in principle the church is the representative of the Kingdom of God; he is wrong in overlooking the fact—which as a Catholic he could scarcely help overlooking—that the demonic powers can penetrate into the church itself, both in its doctrines and institutions. He is right to the extent in which he emphasizes the demonic element in every political structure of power. He is wrong to the extent in which he neglects the creative significance of the political power for historical existence.

III

In the symbol of the Kingdom of God the final victory over the demonic powers in existence generally and in history especially is implied.

The Kingdom of God is a dynamic conception. It designates the necessity that the ultimate meaning of existence is never given; it acquires reality only in overcoming meaninglessness and the distortion of meaning. "Righteousness, peace, and joy," the characteristics of the Kingdom, enclose a possible opposition which is overcome in them. It is not completed but always becoming; not present, neither immanently nor transcendently, but always "at hand." It expresses that "God is a living God," entering history, struggling in history, fulfilling history and is not the unity of eternal essences.

Therefore it is wrong to conceive the Kingdom of God merely as the restoration of the original order which has been destroyed by sin. We know nothing of such an order. It is an abstraction whose roots lie in a static conception of transcendence. The Kingdom of God is, however, not a system of eternal essentialities, whose realization was given in the Creation, was lost at the Fall, and was regained in Redemption. The Kingdom of God is the dynamic fulfillment of the ultimate meaning of existence against the contradictions of existence.

Part Two: The General Christian Principles

The Kingdom of God as the Meaning of History

I

For the Christian consciousness Christ is the center of history. His appearance is interpreted as the "fullness of time," that is, as the fulfillment of all historical preparation.

In calling Christ the center of history we do not apply a general category to a special case, but we apply a category which is found through the analysis of the significance of Christ (in Christian faith) to Christ; we return to Christ what we have taken from him. For in Christ, namely in the reality which is contained in different original interpretations in the New Testament, Christianity sees the appearance of the ultimate meaning of life in history. The fact that the Christian nations speak of a period before and a period after Christ shows how deeply Christian consciousness is penetrated by belief in Christ as the center of history.

The center of history is decisive for the beginning and the end of history. From the Christian point of view history has a suprahistorical beginning—the Fall; and an intrahistorical beginning—the rise of the expectation of a redeeming event. History has also a suprahistorical end—the final consummation or the parousia of

Christ; and it has an intrahistorical end—the victory over the antidivine powers which arise in history, or the Reign of Christ. Neither this beginning nor this end can be determined in terms of physical time. We can express them only in symbolic records of the past (Gen. 1–12) and in symbolic interpretations of the future (millenniums).

A specially important category of the New Testament interpretation of history is kairos. It designates the fulfillment of the period of expectation or preparation, and the beginning of the period of reception or fragmentary actualization. The Greek word *kairos,* which originally only meant without discrimination the "right time," is used in a prophetic interpretation of history for *the* right time in which all time gains its meaning and qualification. The predominance of the logos doctrine within the Greek church prevented the development of a kairos doctrine: that is, a Christian interpretation of history.

II

The Christian interpretation of history considers the history of mankind ultimately as history of salvation.

The belief that Christ is the center of history, and that in him the reality of salvation has appeared in history, implies the belief that human history is ultimately to be interpreted in terms of salvation. Salvation means the fulfillment of what existence ought to be by overcoming the destructive, meaning-defying powers of existence. As in Christian doctrine, Christ is saving humanity in life as well as beyond temporal life, so the history of salvation is going on in history as well as beyond history. Salvation is actualized in history whenever a demonic power in social or individual existence is overcome by the divine power which has become visible in Christ. And salvation is actualized beyond history in the ultimate unification and purification of meaning.

The human mind is not able to conceive salvation beyond life and history in terms taken from world experience which are technically called "ontic." It can be conceived only in terms of meaning. If ontic terms such as resurrection, immortality, new earth, and new heaven are used, they have a symbolic character, since they point to some elements of the ultimate meaning of existence. So, for instance, the symbol of resurrection points to the truth that the totality of personal life, including the human body, belongs to the ultimate meaning of existence. The symbol of a new earth points to the truth that the natural basis of history is not excluded from the ultimate meaning of existence. Hence it follows that the choice of symbols is decisive for truth or error.

Salvation is related to individuals as well as to groups, to mankind as well as to nature, to personalities as well as to institutions. For the problem of history the salvation of groups and institutions is of special importance. It means that the demonic perversion and destruction of groups and institutions is overcome, partially in history, completely beyond history. While the Christian churches in the Catholic period dealt with the salvation of individuals and with the salvation of groups and institutions only with respect to the church itself, and in Protestantism the salvation of groups and institutions is neglected altogether, the post-Protestant period of Christianity probably will deal predominantly with the ultimate meaning and the salvation of groups and institutions. The fact that a religious interpretation of history has become a very urgent problem of applied theology testifies to this.

The Kingdom of God in History

I

The realization of the Kingdom of God within history is determined by the history of the church, in part directly through the historical growth of the church itself, and partly indirectly through the conscious or unconscious relation of all history to the history of the church.

If the meaning of history is salvation, then all history must be related to that course of history in which redemption is prepared and received. The church is the "bearer" of this course of history, both in the stage of preparation and in the stage of deception.

Hence we are justified in calling the church the "bearer" of history. Of course this does not mean that the events of world history have been determined, in a historico-empirical sense, by the synagogue and the Christian churches; only a very small part of mankind, from the point of view of space and time, has any contact with the churches at all, and even where there is contact, or even very close touch, it is truer to say that the secular powers have far more influence on the outward destiny of the churches than the other way round. But the church is more than the Christian churches and their precursors. The church is the community of those partly visible and partly invisible, who live in the light of the ultimate meaning of existence, whether in expectation or in reception. The church, understood in this way, is the power which gives meaning to historical life as a whole.

The meaning of Christian missions is based upon this truth. It is the task of the Christian mission to gather the potential, divided church out of all religions and cultures and to lead it into the actual church, and in so doing to transform potential world history into actual world history to give humanity a unified historical consciousness. This also means that all over the world expectation is to be transformed into reception.

II

Through Christ as the center of history, history is divided into two main periods: the period of preparation and the period of expectation. In each of these two main periods, however, this division is repeated, insofar as history always has the basic character either of expectation or of reception and fragmentary actualization of a new principle of meaning. The transition from the one to the other may be called a special kairos.

From the standpoint of its ultimate meaning all history is either the preparation for or the reception of the center of history. But the preparation is never merely preparation; it is always also anticipating actualization.

If it were not so, all pre-Christian history would be devoid of meaning. But this would be true neither of the prophetic Hebrew stage of preparation nor of the general "sacramental" preparation within paganism. The vital force of both is drawn from their anticipating reception of the center of history; the Jewish development in direct preparation for its appearance, and the pagan development in indirect preparation create the parallelity of understanding. On the other hand, the post-Christian development is never only reception, since it always contains pagan and Jewish elements of expectation and preparation.

The fundamental division applies also to the two main periods themselves. Each period is subdivided into shorter periods, each with its own center which gives it meaning, its own beginning and end. Periods which seem to be controlled by expectation are succeeded by periods which prove to be a fragmentary actualization. From the sociological point of view this has been described as the rhythm of "critical" and "organic" periods. Even the history of the church often follows this course. But no age is completely lacking in "reception" and none is without an element of "expectation."

For the Christian interpretation of history the centers of particular periods are dependent upon the center of history. This gives the criterion for the interpretation of each center and for historical universal action from every particular center. If the New Testament idea of the kairos is applied within a definite period, it expresses the conviction that that which has appeared once for all in "the fullness of time" has reappeared in a special way as the center of a particular historical period. The unique, nonrecurring kairos remains the standard for all the particular forms in which it reappears. For instance, the period preceding the Reformation may be called a period of expectation and anticipating actualization. The appearance of the new interpretation of the center of history by Luther may be called a special kairos (as Luther himself felt), and the Protestant materialization after him may be called a period of reception and fragmentary actualization. In the same way the present period of the decay of liberalism and secularism may be called a period of expectation, which perhaps may be followed by a period of reception after the turning point, the kairos, has occurred. It is exactly this feeling which gave rise to the renewal of the doctrine of kairos by religious socialism. It is impossible to give criteria abstracted from the actual situation by which the existence or nonexistence of a special kairos can be judged. It is a matter of the faith of those who act in a special situation; it is a venture which may fail because faith and spiritual power may not be strong enough. The "will of God" in any given historical situation cannot be recognized by general criteria but only by daring faith.

Salvation and World History

I

For the Christian interpretation of history salvation is the meaning of world history. But salvation is not the same thing as world history. Primarily and above all salvation is judgment passed upon world history.

The negative presupposition of world history is human freedom with which the symbol of Temptation deals, and the emergence of the contradiction between essence and existence which is expressed in the symbol of the Fall. From this presupposition of history there follows the contradiction in which it stands to salvation: salvation is the actual overcoming of the contradiction between essence and existence upon which world history is based.

A direct expression of the contradiction in history is the abuse of power. Power in itself is a structural principle of historical existence. But it is not only in accordance with but also in opposition to the meaning which is to be realized through historical power. It not only fulfills historical vocation but it also betrays it. Insofar as all history is a history of struggles for power, salvation is judgment passed on world history. The external expression of this judgment is the destruction of power by power. Hence in the Kingdom of God, the goal of world history, power is only found in absolute unity with love.

II

If world history were only opposition to salvation, it would directly destroy itself. It can only exist at all because it is not only judged by salvation but is also supported by it.

Power cannot exist without a meaning, in the name of which it is power. The values with which power must unite itself are realizations of the meaning of history, moments in the fragmentary actualization of salvation upon which the possibility of power, and therefore of history, are based. The sociological expression for the fact that power needs a meaning, in order to be able to exist, is "ideology." The word "ideology" has acquired a negative sense, challenging the deliberate or unconscious misuse of ideas for the preservation of a power whose existence is threatened. But the thing itself, the combination of power and value, should not be estimated in a merely negative manner; it is the positive foundation of history as a whole.

History is carried by those groups and individuals who represent in their existence a meaning which belongs to the ultimate meaning and is unified and purified in it. As far as salvation is the latent meaning of history, those are its real bearers who incorporate and represent in themselves this meaning, either in expectation or in reception. The spirit of salvation radiating from those personalities and groups is the power which again and again overcomes the demonic self-destruction of historical existence. If we call the latent community of those people the invisible church, we must agree with the New Testament in asserting that the church is the real bearer of history. This is not a claim for the empirical churches, but a demand upon them.

It is a general experience that in the moment in which the divine breaks into the temporal and a new kairos is approaching the demonic acquires increased power. It is, however, impossible to derive from this experience a general law of progressive-regressive development of universal history. Both judgments, the optimistic as well as the pessimistic, should be avoided.

III

As salvation is carrying world history so, on the other hand, world history is the fragmentary actualization of salvation.

The seriousness and the gravity of human history depends upon the fact that world history is the fragmentary actualization of salvation. Each particular act which is related to the ultimate meaning which has appeared in Christ has infinite significance, because it is the "coming of the Kingdom of God." It is a logical result of their point of view that those who interpret the Kingdom of God in a purely transcendental manner finally come to regard history as a meaningless occupation of man with himself, while the concept of salvation falls away altogether.

The fragmentary actualization of salvation in world history does not mean that salvation can be fulfilled within history. For salvation within history is opposed by destruction; the divine is opposed by the demonic. Salvation is actual within world history to the extent in which the destructive forces are overcome, the power of the demonic is broken, and the final fulfillment of meaning appears. Thus salvation within world history does not remove the conflict between the divine and the demonic.

Accordingly the doctrine of the millennium should not be interpreted as a static final condition, and certainly not in Augustine's sense of the sovereignty of the hierarchy. The millennium should be interpreted as the symbol of the victory over concrete demonic forces within history. The demonic is subdued in actual victories from time to time—but it is not extirpated. When the power of a particular form of the demonic is broken the kairos of a particular period is fulfilled. To expect not only that the power of concrete demonic forces will be broken at definite periods in history, but that in some future age the demonic as a whole will be utterly destroyed, is a religious utopianism which should be regarded as quite untenable.

The relationship of the fragmentary actualization of salvation in history and its fulfillment in the transcendent unity and purity of meaning cannot be expressed in terms of time and history. Every attempt to do so makes the ultimate meaning a section in the totality of meanings, a history after history, a time after time. History itself can define the suprahistorical only in negative terms. Every positive expression is a symbol and has to be understood as such in order to avoid that "transcendent utopianism" which belongs to the distortions of religion and Christianity.

Part Three: The Present Tasks of the Christian Interpretation of History

The Significance of the "Present" for the Christian Interpretation of History

I

Historical interpretation is self-reflection on the part of one who is acting historically about the meaning, the purpose, and the presuppositions of his historical action. The Christian interpretation of history is the reflection of the Christian who acts as a member of the church about the meaning, the purpose, and the presuppositions of his action as a member of the church.

Historical interpretation is *self*-interpretation, that is to say, the historical interpreter must himself be living and acting historically. History cannot be understood from the outside, from the nonhistorical point of view of the spectator. All historical interpretation contains a concrete historical decision; that is, the spectator's point of view has been abandoned. Historical action is not confined to political action in the narrower sense of the word. All action which aims at the formation of community, however theoretical it may be, is historical action; in the broadest sense of the word it is "political."

The purpose of this process of reflection on the part of one who is acting historically is to help him to perceive the spiritual presuppositions on which his action is based and further, by the give-and-take of discussion with those who hold views, either to justify, or, if necessary, to alter his own basic principles, and thus to give spiritual weight and the power to create community to historical action.

All this also applies to the Christian interpretation of history, which is self-reflection on the spiritual presuppositions of the action of the church; for Christian-historical action is church action. Reflection on the part of one who is acting as a member of the church is reflection upon his spiritual presuppositions, that is, the spiritual principles, the essential philosophical and theological ideas, and the present reality from which his action springs.

Church action flows in two directions: along one channel it seeks to influence the churches which now exist as historical facts, along the other channel church action is directed toward the historical existence of an epoch as a whole.

II

All Christian historical action is determined on the one hand by the universal center of history, and on the other by the center of the particular period in which the action takes place. Accordingly, in all Christian historical action the sense of the unique kairos is combined with the sense of a special realization of this kairos; this also implies that the struggle against the demonic forces in general becomes concrete in the struggle against the particular demonic phenomena of the present day.

Christian historical action or church action, in the universal sense of the word, is bipolar: the one pole is the unique *(einmalige)* center of history, the kairos in which in principle the ultimate meaning of history has appeared, in which the demonic destruction of history has in principle been broken. The other pole is the actual situation from which the action of the church springs, whether such action is related to the churches themselves or to historical existence as a whole.

"Church action," in this sense, may take the form of ecclesiastical politics or the politics of the state, it may be theological or philosophical, artistic or liturgical work, or it may take the form of constructive work in religious or secular communities, education in church or school. Every actual situation from which Christian historical action proceeds contains a negative and a positive element: the negative element is the special demonic phenomenon which is characteristic of a period, and especially of a period of transition, and against which the prophetic struggle of the church must be directed; the positive element is the special promise and the special demand which this situation carries with it, an element which was described by the term kairos.

The bipolarity of Christian historical action, as well as the difference between its two tendencies, is the cause of a whole series of tensions and problems which arise out of a one-sided emphasis on one of these poles or on one of these tendencies. If the unique kairos excludes every other, that is, if it denies bipolarity, then all Christian historical action becomes meaningless: the reality of the Kingdom of God is independent of such action, for it belongs to a sphere beyond and above history (dialectical theology). If the individual concrete forms of the kairos destroy the unique kairos, then the criterion for Christian historical action disappears, and in place of the struggle against the demonic we see Christian theology falling a prey to changing forms of the demonic (nationalistic theology). If one-sided emphasis is laid upon the tendency to concentrate action *within* the church, then world history itself is abandoned, uncriticized, to the dominion of that force which destroys all meaning (orthodox Lutheran theology). If one-sided emphasis is laid on Christian historical action outside the church, then church history loses its independence, and in so doing its critical power to give meaning to history as compared with world history (liberal-reformed and denominational theology).

Christian historical or ecclesiastical action is carried out either by the church as such, that is, by its official representatives (synods, bishops, clergy, lay people who exercise official ecclesiastical functions), or by members of the church (under some circumstances also outside the organized churches) who act as members of the church but not as representatives of the church. Representative ecclesiastical action may be directed both negatively and positively toward the church itself (creation of confessions or creeds and of constitutions, fight against heresies and wrong conditions), but it can only influence historical existence outside the church negatively, not positively (by revealing the demonic forces and their destructive consequences, by forming a critical estimate of ideas and plans in the light of the ultimate standard, but not by fighting for definite philosophical, artistic or political solutions). The positive aspect of historical action outside the church can only be achieved by Christians who are either entirely or in certain definite functions not representative of the church, and who are willing to incur the risk of falling into philosophical and political errors, and of being disowned by the church (Christian philosophers, educationists, politicians, artists, etc.). The Christian interpretation of history which issues from the sphere of concrete historical decisions of this kind has no ecclesiastical or dogmatic significance, but it may have prophetic or theological significance.

The Actual Demonic Forces of the Present Day

I

The fundamental demonic phenomenon of the present day is the autonomy of the capitalistic economic system, with all its contradictions, and the mass disintegration and destruction of meaning in all spheres of historical existence which it produces. This demonic force has been unmasked in the main by the prophetic spirit outside the church, but this discovery may, and indeed must, be absorbed into Christian historical categories and developed still further; we should also note that the Christian interpretation of history given in this article owes some of its own vital impulses to this discovery of capitalism as a demonic force.

The autonomy of the economic sphere, which is the result of the doctrine of economic liberalism, has had two fundamental results: first of all, it has caused the class struggle which arises inevitably out of the mechanism of an industrial system, which like all other demonic forces is quite independent of the moral will of the individual and causes destructive divisions within society, and even within the church. Second, the economic sphere, which has become autonomous, has brought all the other spheres of human historical life into subjection to itself and has deprived them of independent meaning; thus it has set in motion a great process of mass disintegration, the movement of which is subject to destructive laws.

The socialist movement, and primarily theoretical Marxism, has opened the eyes of Western society to the working of these laws. The vitally prophetic element in Marxism, under the pressure of the spiritual situation of the nineteenth century, has clothed itself in antireligious materialistic forms, which are inadequate for what is meant by the idea of socialism. Under the name of "religious socialism" the Christian interpretation of history has set itself the task of expressing the antidemonic criticism of Marxism in the categories of the Christian interpretation of history; the impulse to the discovery of such categories came essentially out of the presence of a socialistic movement with a Marxist interpretation of history: the categories which are expounded in this article have been brought into the sphere of the theological thought of the present day by the urge to unite Christianity and socialism in positive criticism.

The content of the categories of the Christian interpretation of history springs from the prophetic and sectarian tradition and its reflection on the philosophy of history throughout the centuries. Christian theology, which makes these categories its own, does not support a special political party, but by making use of the intellectual tool which a sociological theory has placed at its disposal it has reformulated Christian thought on history. The implicit political decision which has been made in religious socialism cannot become an ecclesiastical decision in the formal sense of the word. It must remain a venturesome decision of some individual members of the church, a decision which may possibly contain error. The church, however, is under obligation to bear formal witness against the destructive consequences of the demonic forces of the present day and their heretical foundations.

II

The demonic force of nationalism is dependent on the demonic element in the economic system, yet at the same time, as a means of mass reintegration, it is to some extent opposed to it. At the present time nationalism is the most evident and the most dangerous incarnation of the demonic principle in general, especially where, as in various places, it has assumed an explicitly religious form. It represents the modern variety of polytheistic bondage to space and division, and it drives that section of mankind which has fallen under its sway to historical self-destruction.

Nationalism means that the natural and historical reality known as the "nation" is posited as an absolute: that is, it constitutes the Supreme Good to all who belong to it. This also means that all who do not belong to this nation are excluded from a share in this Supreme Good. To the prophetic view of history the Supreme Good and the criterion of all historical existence is the Kingdom of God, in which all national divisions have been removed, but to nationalism the self-assertion of the nation over against every other is the Supreme Good and the criterion by which human historical existence is measured. Thus in nationalism the emphasis upon space, characteristic of polytheism, has been restored, in contrast to the emphasis on time in prophetic and Christian monotheism.

Nationalism must therefore be described as neopaganism even when it assumes no explicitly religious form. In the countries in which it has assumed a religious form the Christian and the nationalistic views of history have come into open conflict, and the church has formally condemned nationalistic neopaganism as

heretical and demonic. The Christian interpretation of
history, however, must go further and reveal the
heretically demonic character of the nationalistic system of values as such; above all it must show that with
the elevation of a definite space, of a definite race, and
of a definite nation to the rank of the Supreme Good,
history as such has been abandoned, spatial coordina-
tion and division have triumphed over temporal direction towards a goal.

The development of nationalism in the Christian
West is made possible by the division and disintegration
introduced by capitalism. Once the nation had been
substituted for the church as a unifying center, it appeared to afford the first and the most natural principle
of reintegration; this process was hastened by the fact
that the church was utterly incapable of providing such
a principle, since she was weakened by her own divisions and by the fact that she too was entangled in the
net of widespread disintegration. But this nationalistic
form of reintegration, when regarded from the Christian and the humanistic point of view (which indeed
overlap), actually represents the most advanced stage
of disintegration. Nationalism must be unmasked and
attacked by those who hold the Christian and prophetic
view of history as a kind of false prophecy in the sense
of the Old Testament.

III

The necessity for the reintegration of the masses has led
to dictatorial forms of government, in which the demonic force of an unrestricted exercise of power drives
men into presumption toward God and to destruction
of the human values which belong to the Kingdom of
God: formal justice, truthfulness, and freedom. This is
also true of that form of government which, in the
name of material justice, has rejected the demonic
forces of capitalism and nationalism.

Unrestricted exercise of power is a demonic temptation which none who possess it can resist. The early
church expressed this in its condemnation of the
Roman Empire. Henceforward tyranny has always

evoked the opposition of Christian historical thought. Tyranny is presumption toward God and oppression of man. Hence it falls under the condemnation of that combination of love and power represented by the idea of the Kingdom of God.

This is the case, in the first place, when dictatorship is surrounded by a halo of an almost religious kind, or when it proceeds to attack the church. The deification of the dictator, whether as the representative of the ruling power or as an individual; the interference of the state, with its totalitarian claims, with the sphere of religion; the quasi-religious character of its decrees imposed like taboos; the enforced conformity of the church to the state, or its destruction; and the creation of martyrs in the narrower sense of the word—these are the anti-Christian implications of the exercise of absolute power. They force the churches into a campaign of direct resistance, and they provoke those who hold the Christian and prophetic view of history to make a vigorous protest against this demonic exercise of power.

But there is another series of results of the unrestricted exercise of power which also comes under the condemnation of the idea of the Kingdom of God: the destruction of human values by tyranny. The Christian doctrine of man and woman as created in the image of God, as well as the doctrine of Christ as the Logos, means that Christianity is responsible for the human values: formal judicial justice, which is the prophetic standard for the estimate of a political power; truthfulness, to deny which the New Testament regards as an evident sign of the satanic principle; and freedom, that is, the recognition of human dignity or, in Christian terms, the fact that every human being is potentially a child of God. To the satanic principle also the New Testament ascribes all actions which injure this human dignity, whether they touch man's mental life (by putting a stumbling block in his way) or his physical life (by murder).

The deliberate renewal of these demonic forces, whose power has already been broken by Christianity in principle and is being hotly contested by Christian humanism in practice, constitutes the third outstanding "sign of the times." Even the Bolshevist dictatorship, in spite of the fact that it is fighting against capitalistic and nationalistic disintegration in the name of material justice, is of this demonic character. Thus the protagonists of the Christian view of history are called to bear their testimony in the name of the idea of the Kingdom of God, in the midst of their present historical existence, against capitalism, from the point of view of its content; against nationalism, on account of its content and its way of exercising authority; and against Bolshevism on account of its way of exercising authority.

The Kairos of the Present Moment

I

The demonic, in a threefold form, threatens to destroy our present historical existence. From the human point of view the tragic element in this situation drives those who study history from the Christian point of view to inquire into the positive meaning of these events: that is, the kairos immanent within the present moment in history. In accordance with the double direction of ecclesiastical action a double answer is required: one which is given within the church and one outside the borders of the church.

A situation is tragic in which the very elements which are most valuable by their very value drive it to self-destruction. This is the case with the humanistic element contained in capitalism, as well as with the purpose of reintegration which is contained in nationalism, and with the expectation of justice which is contained in Bolshevism. All three in a tragic fate contradict their own original intention and are driving society as a whole, in the Christian West, toward self-destruction. The protagonists of the Christian view of history cannot prevent this tragic fate, but they can and should show clearly the kairos which is being fulfilled within this process of self-destruction, that is, the positive principle which is giving meaning to this development. In so doing they will provide the present action

of the church with a concrete criterion and a concrete
aim for the future.

II

The fact that our present historical existence is
menaced means that the church is called to reformu-
late the universal reintegrating principle which Christianity contains, the center of history as a whole and as
a present center. Negatively, this means the freeing of
the church from her entanglement with the disintegrating powers of the present and the past; positively,
it means the preparation of a new historical existence
through the action of the church.

It is impossible in this connection to point to all the
consequences which spring from the Christian action of
the church within her own borders. Some points only
can be mentioned here.

First of all we must understand the radical nature of
the present process of historical self-destruction, in
which the churches also are involved. This applies to
Protestantism in particular, with its lack of power to
provide a reintegrating principle for the masses. We
must reckon with the possibility that, in the narrower
sense of the word, the Protestant period of the church
may already be ended, in order to make way for a new
post-Protestant form of Christianity. In this time of
change in her own life and in historical existence as a
whole the church must strengthen her own life and
must also transcend it. She strengthens herself by a
deep and thorough union with that center of history
which she proclaims and by which she lives. It is at the
moment that she makes room for historical change that
she needs the criterion by which all history is to be
judged. The act of transcending herself is based upon
the knowledge that there is an invisible history of the
church, for which the visible churches are also responsible, and by which at the same time they are determined.

For the action of the church from within her own
borders the special kairos of this period will consist in

the preparation of a historical existence of her own
after the self-destruction of the present structure of
historical existence. This process of preparation includes three elements: being set free from entanglement with the disintegrating demonic forces of present
history, fresh consideration of the ultimate criterion as
compared with history as a whole, and the application
of this criterion to ecclesiastical action both inside and
outside the church.

III

So far as the action of the church outside her own borders is concerned, the present menace to historical existence summons her to represent the unity of the
Kingdom of God in face of the divisions caused by the
demonic forces. Where capitalism is concerned this
means the application of the criterion of material justice. Where nationalism is concerned it means the application of the criterion of the unity of the human race.
Where dictatorship is concerned it means the application of the criterion of the finite character, and yet at
the same time the dignity of every human being.

The application of the criterion of justice to the present social situation means the destruction of the capitalistic class contrast and of the autonomous supremacy
of economics over life as a whole. The use of the word
"socialism" to describe this process does not mean a
decision for a special party, but it does mean the concrete character of the demand for justice in the historical situation of disintegrating capitalism.

The application of the criterion of the unity of the
human race to the present international situation
means the removal of the dominating political sovereignty of the individual states. The use of the word
"pacifism" for this demand does not mean the support
of the present pacifist organizations, but the concrete
character of the demand for peace in the historical
situation of self-destructive nationalism.

The application of the criterion of the finite character
and yet the dignity of every human being to the present political situation means the introduction of

antidictatorial corrections into the structure of government. The use of the expression "the rights of man" for this demand does not mean the support of a liberalistic structure of society, but the concrete character of the Christian-humanistic demand, in a situation in which tyranny dominates the masses.

IV

It is in accordance with the idea of the kairos that that which the ultimate criterion requires is a promise and therefore an object of hope. And since, from the point of view of history, every promise is connected with the condition of human free activity, the hope of any historical realization remains doubtful. The only unconditional prospect is the promise and expectation of the suprahistorical fulfillment of history, of the Kingdom of God, in which that which has not been decided within history will be decided and that which has not been fulfilled within history will be fulfilled.

The phenomenon which is described in the New Testament as interpretation of the "signs of the times"—the judgment on the "tendencies" of the present which is always presupposed in action—this is meant by the unity of demand and expectation in interpreting history. In every period there are symptoms which show what is going on under the surface. The perception and the interpretation of these symptoms is the task of the prophetic spirit, which may appear either in a more intuitive or in a more rational form, but is never wholly without either the one or the other. The words of Jesus, "Repent, for the kingdom of heaven is at hand," represent in classic form that combination of demand and expectation which arises out of the interpretation of the kairos. The most magnificent theoretical interpretation and the most effective practical interpretation of a historical period was the Marxist analysis of capitalist society. It too united summons and demand with interpretation and expectation.

Historical interpretation from the point of view of the kairos must resist the temptation to separate demand and expectation. Mere demand leads to pharisa-

ism and moralistic utopianism. Just as the Jew who was
loyal to the law found it impossible to bring in the day
of the Lord by force, so in our own day pacifists and
utopian socialists have found it impossible to enforce
world peace and social justice by means of moralistic
propaganda. Only that which at least potentially exists
as a reality can be realized historically. The Kingdom of
God only comes at all because in Christ it is already
"among us." World peace will only come insofar as the
actual union of humanity has in principle removed the
divisions caused by nationalism. The classless society
will only come when the inward power of society has
already been concentrated in *one* class. But all this does
not imply any inevitable course of events. The Kingdom of God "tarries" in the process of drawing mankind together, new "confusions of tongues" break out,
the class in which all classes are to be removed may fail,
or may fall a prey to new divisions.

Neither prophetic promise nor historical dialectic
speaks of things which *must* happen. It is not the
prophet but the diviner, not the dialectician but the
mechanist, who tries to predict the course of history
and thus tries to turn it into a natural process.

The certainty that these elements of demand and
promise which a kairos contains will be fulfilled points
to the suprahistorical unity of the ultimate meaning.
Here, and here only, all that is undecided in history is
decided, and all that is unfulfilled is fulfilled. Therefore
historical action can remain sure of itself, and the religious interpretation of history can defend its rights,
even in face of the disappointment provided by unfulfilled expectation and fragmentary actualization. The
question of history has a final answer: the Kingdom of
God.

2

The Meaning
of Anti-Semitism

As a German philosopher who was forced to leave Germany a few months after the victory of National Socialism because of his religious, philosophical, and political convictions, and as a Christian theologian who has been called to one of the most famous theological institutions of this country, I desire in this hour of shame, repentance, protest, and rededication to speak of the attack on Christianity which is implied in the attack on the Jews and of the destruction of the German mind and soul which is involved in the destruction of Jewish lives and homes.

Few words are required to prove that the struggle for the eradication of Judaism is, in its profoundest meaning, a struggle to eradicate Christianity. There are, of course, minor reasons for it as well, such as economic competition, the inferiority complex of the persecutors, primitive racial instincts, mistakes made on both sides. But all these minor reasons do not explain the greatest and most cruel persecution which has been maintained day by day for the past five years and of which the outbreak of the past weeks was the most visible but by no means the most cruel manifestation. There is more involved in this blind fanaticism which sacrifices prestige, goodwill, and political and economic advantage to achieve its end. A religious issue is involved; for this is a demonic struggle against the God of Abraham and the prophets, who is also the God of Jesus and of St. Paul, of Augustine and of Luther, the God whose holy name is Jehovah, the Lord of Hosts. His name is now to be erased from Christian buildings, hymns, and prayers.

The question is whether the God of Abraham, the God in whom all the nations of the earth are blessed, Germans and Negroes, Chinese and Americans, Russians and Japanese—whether the God of Christ who has brought all natural powers in subjection to himself, blood and soil, race and nation, state and culture— whether the God of the German prophet and reformer Martin Luther, the God whose majesty humbles all human pride and arrogance, both religious and national, the God of righteousness and truth, of charity and humility, shall remain our God; or whether the gods of soil and blood of race and nation shall triumph over him. These gods are not gods but demons destroying themselves and each other, perverting universal justice into caprice and arbitrariness, universal truth into the lies of propaganda, and humility into pride and arrogance wherever they appear in the world, whether in Germany or in Russia, in America as well as in Europe, among Jews or Christians. They have become especially powerful in the present world situation. The persecution of the Jews thus signifies that an era of world history is drawing to its close.

The Christian churches are beginning to realize this. At the ecumenical conference of the churches at Oxford in 1937, national and racial ideology was solemnly condemned as the chief opponent of Christianity today. I would like to say to the Lutheran churches of this nation that I, as a German Lutheran, have some understanding for your hesitation in taking sides in the religious war which rages in Germany. But the tragic events of recent weeks must give you courage to arrive at a more unequivocal Christian decision, a decision in the spirit of Martin Luther, who challenged the anti-Christ wherever he believed him manifested in his own day. You must see that the spirit of Luther lives today not in those who compromise again and again only to be disillusioned but in the uncompromising spirit of such a man as Martin Niemöller, over whose fate the Christian churches are incidentally greatly concerned, more particularly since there is reason to suspect that efforts are now being made to induce a general breakdown in his great mind and personality. In common with all Christian churches I ask my Lutheran friends to make their decision against the demonic powers who would bring Christians and Jews alike to martyrdom.

The decision for which I plead is not a decision against the German people. It is a decision against those who have the German nation in their grip, aided by the irresistible weapons which a technical civilization has fashioned. These forces have been brought to power and maintained in it by the mistakes of postwar politics; by the selfishness of the privileged classes inside and outside Germany; by the impotence, despair, and disintegration of the German masses; by the ignorance and indifference of the average citizen of other nations; by the spiritual weakness among ourselves who were supposed to be the spiritual and intellectual leaders of Germany. Now that they are in power they use their power to create a German empire and to destroy the German soul. For while the persecuted are destroyed physically, the persecutors are destroyed spiritually.

To the American of German descent I should like to say: Do not dare to give the impression that the Germany of these persecutors is that Germany to which you feel loyal in your hearts. If you are loyal to this new Germany you will be disloyal to the true Germany. You would be disloyal to the Germany of universal history, to the Germany of the Middle Ages in its noble and pious unity of Christianity and chivalry; you would be disloyal to the Germany of the Renaissance and humanism, to the Germany of the Reformation with its struggle for the sole majesty of God and for freedom of conscience; you would be disloyal to the Germany which is revealed in the classical periods of her history. Every one of the great Germans whose tombs are desecrated and whose ideas are suppressed today fought for the unity of mankind, for the recognition of the dignity of every human being, and for the victory of justice. Not a few of them were indebted to Jewish teachers, pupils, disciples, interpreters, and friends and there was not one who did not express contempt and opposition for the moral ugliness of anti-Semitism. This is true even of and especially of Friedrich Nietzsche, who is claimed by the present rulers of Germany as their special philosopher but who found the strongest words of all great Germans against the evil resentments of anti-Semitic propaganda which came to the surface just at his time. One could quote the protests of great German literature against tyranny, and the distortion of humanity, for hours. I hope there will be occasion to let this spirit speak in behalf of the true and real Germany at the German exhibition of the New York World's Fair, if the committee of which I have the honor to be chairman succeeds in securing the support of American and European friends for this exhibit, which intends to reveal the Germany of the past and, as we fondly hope, the Germany of the future.

After five years of silence I am speaking for the first time in a political meeting against those who are the real enemies of the German soul, against those who are building an empire but corrupting the kingdom of justice and truth. I wish my speech to be a pledge for the true Germany. No one who has been seduced by the power and who has succumbed to the fascination of the present Germany, no official representative, no compromising mediator could be heard at this moment. Only those who have voiced an uncompromising "no" to the persecuting Germany are able to speak an uncompromising "yes" to the true and persecuted Germany.

May I speak a concluding word to my Jewish friends. It is not idealism but realism which prompts me to voice the consoling assurance that it is not the persecuted but the persecutors who are ultimately destroyed, in their minds and souls. Therefore we must resist the natural and inevitable temptation to bitterness and vindictive passion. Let us not allow ourselves to be cut off from the true Germany, which is today under the heel of persecution. I would not dare to suggest that we persecuted Germans have suffered as you are suffering. Yet we have suffered too. Therefore we must stand united on the ground which is common to prophetic religion, Christianity, and humanism. Let us try to save the fruits which may have ripened in the sad experiences of these days. Not the fruits of hate and separation, for these are poisoned fruits and will be of use only to those whom we are united to oppose; the fruit of this experience which must be preserved is the sense of a new and powerful community of peoples, races, and creeds, transcending their differences and firm in their opposition to anti-Semitic, anti-Christian, and antihumanistic spirit. May this spirit of community, born out of the suffering of the persecuted, become sufficiently strong and creative in time to transform our present world.

3

Spiritual Problems
of Postwar Reconstruction

The presupposition of every postwar reconstruction is
the knowledge of the prewar disintegration. And the
presupposition of every spiritual postwar reconstruction is the knowledge of the spiritual prewar disintegration. Nobody can doubt that a catastrophe such as the
present one never could have happened in an integrated social system; nobody should attribute our period of world wars and world revolutions to the
accident of a special national character, for instance of
the Russian or the German or the Japanese character,
or to the even more accidental rise of dictatorial types
in persons like Stalin or Hitler. It should be granted by
all those who are able to judge that something was
fundamentally wrong in the system of life and thought
in the immediate past and that a return to it is neither
desirable nor possible. The World War is a part of a
world revolution. This statement should be repeated
again and again. Many economists and political scientists have shown the causes of the disintegration in their
respective realms. Philosophers and historians have
given comprehensive pictures of this process, and these
have been confirmed by subsequent events. The spiritual disintegration of the bourgeois society was fore-
seen as early as the middle of the nineteenth century
by Russian religious thinkers and has been restated by
Nicolas Berdyaev and others, supported by ideas of
Nietzsche and Spengler. It was the chief topic in the
German and French literature of the turn of the century. It has been developed in a combination of Marxist

and religious ideas by the movements of religious socialism in Europe and America.

It is obvious that the spirit, the creative, dynamic power of the soul, is not a matter of construction. If spirit is lacking no construction can possibly produce it. It either is or is not active, in individuals or in groups. But if it is active, it creates a body for itself through which it can be manifested and act. Words, forms of life and social institutions, works of culture and religious symbols are the embodiments of the spirit. And these are subject to conscious cultivation and reconstruction. We refer to them when we speak of "spiritual reconstruction after the war."

Any task of spiritual reconstruction has two sides. Those trends in a spiritual development which can stand criticism from the point of view of the ultimate criteria of thinking and acting must be supported and maintained. Spiritual tendencies should not be accepted simply because they belong to a given historical structure—as positivism holds. Neither should general principles be imposed on a spiritual situation which has no organ of receiving them—as idealism attempts. Much wisdom is needed to avoid these two mistakes, which threaten every reconstruction. The second task, equally important, is the protection of the creative trends of the spirit against distortion and corruption. With respect to the spirit of the Asiatic nations and largely with respect to Russia, this protective task is practically the only one which is demanded of us. The Anglo-Saxon countries cannot be responsible for the spiritual reconstruction of Asia (except perhaps indirectly through the effect of contact with the West). The protecting side of the work of spiritual reconstruction is equally important in relation to Europe, including the Axis countries. It would be a tremendous mistake if the victorious democracies intended to impose their own forms and standards of spiritual life on the conquered countries in the name of universal principles. Europe, including Germany, will accept what it is ready to accept according to the dynamics of its own spiritual development, but nothing else. The demand

just made by a resentful German refugee writer that an
army of foreign teachers should be sent to Germany
after the war with the purpose of transforming the German spirit is the most certain way of preventing any
spiritual reconstruction. Nothing spiritual can be given
to the human spirit for which it is not prepared.

The Analysis

The spiritual disintegration of our day consists in the
loss of an ultimate meaning of life by the people of
Western civilization. And with the loss of the meaning
of life, they have lost personality and community. They
have become, whether they know it or not, parts of an
objective process which determines their lives in every
respect from their economic situation to their spiritual
form. The insecurities and the vicissitudes involved in
this process have produced feelings of fear, anxiety,
loneliness, abandonment, uncertitude, and emptiness.
Their spiritual life oscillates between a cynical and a
fanatical surrender to powers, the nature of which nobody can fully grasp or control, and the end of which
nobody can foresee. In the younger generation of Germany, for instance, cynicism prevailed before National
Socialism turned into fanaticism. Today the youngest
group in Germany is returning again to cynicism. Germany for reasons of the loss of the last war was an
extreme case. But anyone who has contact with the
younger generation in Western Europe, and even in
America, in the years between the two wars must have
been impressed and disturbed by their frankly admitted nihilism. This is not surprising. If human beings feel
that their destiny is taken out of their hands, that an
objective process on which they have no influence
throws them on the street today, draws them into a big
machine as parts and tools of tomorrow, and will drive
them into a war of extinction the day after tomorrow,
then no result other than utter hopelessness can be
expected. The goddesses of the later ancient world—
"Tyche and Heimarmene," chance and fate—have
again conquered a civilization and driven millions of
people into resigned surrender to forces beyond their

imagination. This entails and at the same time presupposes the loss of personality as well as of the community. The loss of personality was prepared in the naturalistic philosophy of the bourgeois society and found its final expression in the vitalistic and pragmatic dissolution of the self leading to a psychology without psyche and a doctrine of many without a human ego. But these theoretical developments—to which strict analogies in literature and art can be found—have become historical forces only because they were the natural expression of the actual depersonalization of man. The technical form of monopolistic production, not only of material but also of spiritual goods, has made the individual, both in his production and in his consumption, a part of an all-embracing machine moved by anonymous forces. While in Europe the mechanization of production was more visible, in America the mechanization of consumption is the most characteristic symptom of this situation. It has created not only standardized machines but also standardized human beings conditioned by radio, movies, newspapers, and educational adjustment for a subpersonal fitness to this immense process. The easiness with which, in the dictatorial countries as well as in America, the whole productive machine, including its human tools, has been brought into a unity for one purpose—the war—shows its completely impersonal and meaningless character.

The loss of personality is interdependent with the loss of community. Only personalities can have community. Depersonalized beings have social interrelations. They are essentially lonely and therefore they cannot bear to be alone, because this would make them conscious of their loneliness, and with it, of the loss of meaning of life. The striking "lack of privacy" is not an expression of community but of the lack of community. And there is no community because there is nothing to have in common. The monopolistic direction of public communication of leisure, pleasure, learning, sex relations, sport, etc., does not provide a basis for a real community. Cultural remnants of earlier periods are used to cover up our cultural nakedness. All this is carried through more radically in the totalitarian systems.

But the means of carrying it through are better developed in this country. And if these means ever should come into the hands of unchecked dictators—visible or invisible ones—a complete dehumanization would have even more chances in America than in Europe. The loss of personality and community is the consequence of the loss of an ultimate meaning of life. This has occurred in a development of Western civilization which can be divided into three periods. In the first period, roughly identical with the Early and High Middle Ages, the meaning of life was represented by the transcendent symbols and functions of the church, which gave the foundation for personality as well as for community. The personality was established by its direct relation to the Ultimate, in guilt and salvation. The eternal meaning of the individual self was guaranteed. The community was established by the participation of every group, according to its special vocation, in the symbols of the universal community. A content for community existed out of which the spiritual life could draw inexhaustible material for cultural creation. It is important for our task of a spiritual reconstruction to keep this period in mind because it has become the standard of criticism and the model of demand for many analysts of the present situation, not only for Catholics. Although personality and community were guaranteed in this period, they were not really developed. The transcendent foundation and its representatives on the top of the hierarchy kept them strictly within the limits of the given system and suppressed as long as possible the autonomous creativity of the individual. When this proved impossible, the second period, roughly identical with the rise and victory of bourgeois society, started. Now reason and its metaphysical and ethical creations replaced or transformed the transcendent foundation of life and its symbols. The spiritual production became personal—in religion through Protestantism, in arts and sciences through the Renaissance. It still lived from the substance of the past and, therefore, it still was able to create culture and to maintain community. The so-called classical periods of the European nations are based on this union of free

creation and God-formed substance. In this their greatness and their short transitory character were rooted.
The harmony of individuality and community, which
was guaranteed in the first period by the common foundation of both, survived in the second period as natural
harmony guaranteed by the basic conformity of the
interests and ideologies of the rising bourgeoisie. But
there was, so to speak, an undercurrent in the spiritual
development of bourgeois society, an element of antira-
tional naturalism and pessimism which came to the surface again and again, and which became victorious in
the third period. The spiritual heritage was more and
more wasted; the autonomous creations became more
formalistic, more skeptical, and less universal. The harmony between the individual and the whole broke
down. Community was replaced by cooperation for
purposes; personality, by a quantity of working power
or by technical intelligence and adjustment. In the
meantime, the economic and technical process had
prepared the monstrous mechanism which has swallowed personality as well as community and with them
a spiritual culture. The third period, roughly identical
with monopoly, capitalism, and fascism, had come into
existence.

These are sketchy indications, much too short for a
complete and convincing picture. There is immense
material in all realms of life, the use of which would
make this picture concrete and irrefutable. This, however, is impossible in the given space. But it would have
been utterly unacceptable to speak pleasantly and
hopefully about the postwar reconstruction without the
weight and seriousness which only can be gained by an
analysis of the background of our spiritual disintegration. Perhaps it will be said that the elements pointed
to are only elements but not the whole, and that an
unbalanced stress is laid on them by this analysis. To
this the answer is, first, that there are indeed other
elements and that without these other elements this
article, for instance, would not have been written; second, that the complexity of every historical situation
does not obscure the decisiveness of some trends. These
dominant trends carry the dynamics of the whole. It is

these trends with which we have dealt. Third, it must
be said that the analysis of the self-destructive nature of
bourgeois society always has been rejected and always
has proved to be even truer than the analysts, including
the present writer, were able to believe. The fact of the
Second World War and the self-destruction of European civilization cannot be refuted.

Demands and Possibilities

The abstract statement of the requirements for spiritual reconstruction can simply be derived from the
analysis: the requirement for spiritual reconstruction
after the war is the demand for a convincing restate-
ment of the meaning of life; the discovery of symbols
expressing it; the reestablishment of personality and
community on this new basis. But such a demand includes the demand for an equally radical and inseparable social and political reconstruction. It would, of
course, be foolish to assume that demands like these
have any possibility of immediate actualization. The
catastrophic development of a world war cannot be
wiped out in a peace conference or in a few years of the
education of some evildoers. Nothing sudden can fulfill
the needs resulting from the disintegration of a period
of history. The revolutionary transformation, of which
this war is a part, is a long process in which not even the
forces to be overcome have yet shown their greatest
strength. We are still in what we have called the third
period. The process of centralized mechanization has
not yet reached its final stage. In some countries, as in
America, it has just started. We do not know the possibilities implied in its further progress. There are still
large areas in which structures of the two other periods
have survived. We do not know how far they will be
transformed by the structure of the third period. And
even if the dehumanization, which has taken place
under the reign of monopoly, capitalism, and fascism,
had come to an end, this would not mean a quick rehu-
manization of humanity. Nevertheless, the demands
for spiritual reconstruction, as stated above, are not
meaningless. It is even meaningful to make as many

people as possible realize where they are, what they are missing, what has happened to them, what they have lost, why they are lonely, insecure, anxious, without ultimate purpose, without an ultimate concern, without a real self, and without a real world. Humans are still able to feel that they have ceased to be human. And this feeling is the presupposition of all spiritual reconstruction during and after the war. For in this feeling humanity makes itself heard in its longing for a meaning of life, for community and personality. It has always belonged and still belongs to the great hopes of mankind that as new generations grow up, they may be able to receive new creative germs. The new generations themselves do not produce them; spiritual life presupposes maturity and it spoils the receptive power of the child if it is treated like an adult and is adjusted too early to the given mechanism of social behavior. But fortunately no generation of adults has ever succeeded in imposing its pattern of life completely on the following generation. This is one of the greatest chances for spiritual reconstruction.

The other reason for hope is the fact that the religious and cultural traditions of the earlier periods have survived not only as dead records but, also, as living realities moving and forming individuals and groups. Although the churches as large social institutions have adapted themselves to the great historical transformations—sometimes, as in the Middle Ages and the Reformation, even in a leading role—they have not completely surrendered to the given social structure. They still resist a complete subjection to the trend toward dehumanization and mechanization. But more important, they have preserved the message of an ultimate meaning of life which has not yet been exhausted and which, as Christians believe, never can be exhausted. However, this message can become effective for the coming spiritual reconstruction only if it is brought into the center of the present situation as an answer and not as another problem tied up with the general spiritual disintegration. This cannot be done by the churches officially; it is an adventurous task and the duty of a Christian vanguard of a voluntary and half-

esoteric character. The authority of the churches, especially in their ecumenical unity, may be behind those
who go this way. But the churches themselves are too
much bound by their traditional forms, on the one
hand, and by their amalgamation with the present
structure of society, on the other hand. The support and
protection of a spiritual vanguard will be the main contribution of the churches to the spiritual reconstruction
after the war.

But the churches are not the whole of our culture.
They are only a small sector within an otherwise secular
civilization. Without the participation of the secular
spirit in the work of spiritual reconstruction, nothing
can be done. It is impossible to return to the hierarchical culture of the first period. The autonomous spirit
after having been liberated cannot return into bondage
except by a complete reprimitivization or, as it has
been called by Spengler, "fellahization." Therefore the
spiritual reconstruction demands a cultural vanguard as
much as a religious one. There are personalities in all
realms of life who still represent creative culture, who
have resisted in themselves the trends of mechanization and dehumanization in the name of human dignity
and spiritual values. They have saved their personal self
against the practical naturalism of our existence. But
they were not able to change the situation as such. On
the contrary, they often have become unconscious servants of the dehumanizing process—the character of
which they were not able to understand. Many noble
representatives of the traditions of spiritual culture
served to conceal the barbarism of the social process
which made its way without noticing their ideals at all.
These people, like many religious people, do not even
realize that the second period, which was the period of
classical culture, has gone and that no return to it is
possible. They do not realize that they have become
antiquated in their belief in autonomous culture in our
time. They can become bearers of the spiritual reconstruction only if they join the religious vanguards on the
one hand, the social movements on the other hand.
     Without the collaboration of individuals within the

movements for social justice, no spiritual reconstruction can be conceived of. The most penetrating analysis of the dynamics of bourgeois society has originated from their side. They discovered the loss of community very early and saw the necessity of its replacement by social cooperation. They recognized the strict independence of all elements of a social structure, including the spiritual life. They tried to describe a stage in which the freedom and personality of everybody were guaranteed by the integration of the whole. But they were not able to effect the spiritual reconstruction alone. As mass movements they actually became parts of the whole process against which their protest was directed. They have become, against their will, supporters of the mechanization of life from which they wanted to protect their followers. This is the dialectic to which large historical movements always are subjected, and it shows once more the irresistible power of the main trends of our period. Nevertheless, the social movements at least expressed their protest, often with revolutionary power and a willingness to accept persecution. In unity with the religious vanguards and the bearers of cultural creativity, they will become a source of spiritual reconstruction.

I have not given a program of spiritual reconstruction. It would have been very unspiritual to try it. I have not dealt with the cultural policy of the peace conference and the armies of occupation. This would have been even less spiritual. I have pointed only to the necessity of protecting spiritual creativity against political encroachments. My vision for the spiritual reconstruction of Europe is a large number of anonymous and esoteric groups consisting of religious, humanistic, and socialist people who have seen the trends of our period and were able to resist them, who have contended for personality and community (many of them under persecution), and who know about an ultimate meaning of life even if they are not yet able to express it. The policy of the democracies after the war can only be to protect these groups and spiritual vanguards against political or economic suppression, to use their creativity in the central direction of the world which cannot be avoided for a long time to come. If the victorious governments fail to do so, the spirit will be forced into the underground and no spiritual reconstruction will come forth.

4

Christian Basis of a
Just and Durable Peace

Lecture I: Christian Principles and Political Reality

The special character of this war is that the real problem is not the war but the peace. This is not a normal national war but a war of world revolution under the cover of a war among nations. The real reason for thinking about the peace against all the "First Win the War" slogans is not the practical problem of being ready for peace, it is the question of the meaning of the war. It is not the creation of a program, it is the inner readiness of the people to urge their governments toward peace that is at stake.

The special task of these presentations and of this group is the task of thinking from the point of view of theology. Are there Christian bases for political decisions? If so, in what sense? What does "Christian" mean in this connection? In which ways can the church want to influence political decision? What level of the political decision is open for influence? Who shall represent the influence?

The importance of these questions on the American scene lies in the danger of an unbroken directness of the relation between politics and religion, and from this arise two possibilities. There could be an unbroken negation of the war on the remaining ground of a pacifistic mood. Or there may be an unbroken affirmation of the war. The crusader spirit has been increasingly fed by the war propaganda. There is not much danger of aloofness of religion from the war question, now, in this country. But there is such a danger in Christian theology, and it may become even more dangerous if disappointments occur as they did after the last war.

Therefore we must dedicate ourselves to theological thought in the way of genuine theology, which always was and must be one of the hardest tasks in thinking. We will finish with a transition to the two main problems of a just and durable peace: the social question and the international problem. The first is based on a general analysis of the causes of the war; the second includes the church universal.

The Formal Christian Principles on Which Political Decisions Must Be Made

It is not the Christian doctrine as such but those principles included within it which have a bearing on general and specific political decisions. Differences in understanding these principles create practical differences.

Principles are those ideas involved in Christianity which always determine how a decision is made on the basis of Christianity. It is not special principles but all of them together which are critical. Principles may be seen as formal or material. Formal principles give the way in which the material ones must be applied, or, even more exactly, they prevent a wrong application. They are the critical, the predominantly "Protestant" principles. The others point to the reality of Christian life. But of course they are not independent sets of principles.

1. The principle of the absolute transcendence of the divine.
   a. Its positive meaning is expressed in the first commandment in the majesty and unapproachability of God.
   b. Its negative meaning is the negation of any finite claim to be or to act like God made by finite gods, values, people, groups, or institutions.
   c. Its critical meaning is the challenge against sacramental idolatry as well as against eschatological utopianism—that is, against the claim to embody the divine or to claim to read it in some

future. Progressivism is often a mixture of both and tries in vain to escape the criticism of the first theological principle.

2. The principle of the paradoxical immanence of the divine.
   a. Its positive meaning: Absolute transcendence includes immanence, since no independent opposite can exist. Immanence is paradoxical since transcendence is maintained in it. This is seen in the idea of incarnation in a concrete and universal way. Christ is the reality of this immanence.
   b. Its negative meaning is the negation of a dualistic separation of heaven and hell and of the powerlessness of the divine in history.
   c. Its critical meaning is in the fragmentary and ambiguous character of all historical reality, which is negated by the transcendent principle and paradoxically affirmed by the immanent principle.

3. The principle of the universal reference to the divine.
   a. The positive meaning of this principle is that every reality has a direct relationship to the unconditionally transcendent and paradoxically immanent divine. This is its cosmic character.
   b. The negative meaning is the negation of every limitation of the divine by (1) the exclusion of the secular in deference to the sacred realm, or (2) the exclusion of the spiritual in deference to the bodily realm, or (3) the exclusion of lower sections of reality in deference to the higher ones.
   c. Its critical meaning is threefold: (1) It challenges ecclesiastical and secular arrogance. The emphasis on the church as bearer of the message of paradise in Catholicism is challenged, as is the emphasis on the secular realms as the daily life relationship to God in Protestantism. (2) It challenges the treatment of the interior realm as more divine and the material world as antidi-

vine. This was seen in religious socialism and
Blumhardt's attack on the "inner world" and on
the "material conditions" as the only source of
evil. (3) It protests against mediating hierar-
chies, spiritualistic or nationalistic, and against
an egalitarian negation of election and uniqueness.

The Material Christian Principles
on Which Political Decisions Must Be Based

1. The principle of love as the supporting ground of
reality.
   a. Its nature is to have predominant characteristics—like the principle of transcendence—
   interdependent. Absolute love can be transcendent, immanent, and universal at the same
   time. Its basic character is the movement from
   the one to the complete otherness and the reunion of the remaining otherness. It is the inner
   quality of being as being. It has the element
   of charity, but it is more. It has the
   element of community between individual personalities, but it is more. It is transcendent and
   immanent.
   b. Love would lack political significance if it were
   only a personal feeling added to the general
   structure of power and justice. But it is basic; it
   is the fundamental structure on which the others are dependent. It is the structure of being,
   not a subjective emotion. Therefore the demand of love is not as paradoxical as it would
   seem if love were emotional adherence to a
   person; instead, it is the demand to be what we
   essentially are. That is the concrete application
   of the principle through the two principles of
   life and justice.

2. The principle of life as the dynamic actuality of
being.
   a. The term "living" implies that it is a theological
   principle. This is confirmed by the symbol

"eternal life." But the theological tradition has emphasized eternity against life, especially in Protestantism and rationalistic humanism. The revolt of the life principle is a decisive aspect of the history of the nineteenth and twentieth centuries. Christianity and theology failed to meet the situation. Life is the dynamic position of a center that actualizes itself in continuous interrelation with the whole. The self, as this center, is completed in individual selfhood, which makes a relation to the totality possible, and this includes personality and community or the complete actualization of love in life as the bearer of justice.

But now the danger starts. Life is swallowed by the constant forming of life. Dynamic self-realization is thwarted by static forms and laws. The vital impetus is subjected to moral suppression. Therefore life revolts and power is turned against justice.

This gives an insight into the meaning of power. Life is the dynamic might of the individual center to be. Being is the might of being and of providing actualization to oneself. The center is as powerful as the many elements it can unite in itself. Therefore the absolute power is God and relative powers are communities, etc.

The limits of the power of a being are not given. It is a process of trying, moving forward, going back. The image and limitations of life are not defined. No status quo exists.

b. The political significance of the life principle is its dynamism. First because of love, being expresses its power character in dynamic self-realization. This excludes politics that denies power and demands an idea of justice without power and dynamic uncertainties.

3. The principle of justice as the uniting form of being.

a. Justice is not an abstract law imposed from outside. It is the expression of the substance of being: namely, love. It is not a strange law but an essential law. Therefore it is uniting with the self-realization of life and is not the negation of life. It is neither the guarantee of any status quo nor the guarantee of a powerless utopia. It is in the kairos. Natural law is the principle of justice in relation to life and power. Love actualizes itself in the kairos. This is the unity of life and justice.

    b. Justice is the concrete principle of politics (as universality in the formal sense). But it must be united with the other two principles. Therefore it can never be vindictive justice. It points to the limits in which individual self-realization is compatible with the unity of the whole or with love. It is not egalitarian. It depends on the essentially centralizing power of a group or an individual. Therefore it cannot be separated from power, and both cannot be separated from love. Life without justice is chaos and therefore not the power of being. Justice without life is dead law and therefore strange to being.

In conclusion, the appropriate way of using these principles is not as within a closed system but as standards in concrete, dynamic situations. For example, in India a dynamic justice related to life and power is overcoming status quo politics, and the old order of colonialism is being shaken. The world as a whole is in revolt against the present spiritual and economic situation. The relationship of justice is to the dynamic shaking of the durable. Consequently, the Commission's concepts of "just and durable" are radically in question.

Lecture II: The Social Problem
of a Just and Durable Peace

According to Christian principles the title is problematic. "Just" can only mean fragmentary and ambiguous justice, because justice cannot be separated from life and life is the might of self-realization in a dynamic, tentative way. The same reservation applies to "durable." It means either what "just" means, that is, whatever is adequate to the essential life with power of self-realization, or it means the establishment of a final order, perhaps the order of the status quo. The latter contradicts life and love and is against real justice. It would be the peace of the cemetery. Therefore, instead of these arrogant words, what is required is the realization of the demand involved in the kairos for the concrete unity that is in the trend of life. It is peace according to the actual demands of life. This presupposes an insight into what life demands, an analysis and, perhaps, a prophetic interpretation of its essential trend in its negative and prophetic elements.

The attempted diagnosis is that of a world in revolution. This leaves the emphasis on the social role over against the national roles in the situation.

The Analytic Approach

The great alternatives are the theory of accident and the theory of structural necessity: the first interpretation results in status quo policies; the second results in the fight for a new situation. The former becomes more problematic every day because a heap of ruins is not the basis for a status quo solution. However, at the same time, the latter is the more difficult because visions are a difficult basis for reconstruction. But it must be tried, since the other way is impossible. There is another implication in the alternative. The status quo people emphasize the national role and implicitly even Anglo-Saxon imperialism. The new structure people have seen that the internal situation of practically all nations has created the present situation. "The freedom from want" acknowledges this, but it is too general to include a real decision against the status quo.

The Christian decision cannot be made in the abstract but only on the basis of an analysis. The meaning of social reconstruction is the development in human existence of that species which socially produces and reproduces being with dignity. The social problem never was and never will be the question of an increas-

ing standard of living but of achieving in the realm of
reproduction a situation whereby human potentialities
are not destroyed. Dehumanization is the opposite of
creative life and human self-realization, including the
power of being in personality and community. If reconstruction is impossible, all the material principles of
Christianity are violated. Dehumanization is the term
of the early Karl Marx that was revitalized by religious
socialism and experienced by everybody in Europe between the wars. The question of the social element of
a peace adequate to the kairos is the question of the
establishment of human dignity in the process of collective production.

The analysis itself is based on immense empirical material and an interpretation of material starting in the
middle of the nineteenth century and confirmed by the
development into the First World War. The interpretation itself must be visionary; therefore it participates in
prophecy. It must also give a structural picture.

The Analytic Picture

The relation of reason to nature has been perverted
as reason controlling both nature and the human; this
perversion becomes the ideal of modern liberation.
The belief in harmony between reason and nature was
the belief and impulse of bourgeois society in its fighting and victorious stages. Humanism was the liberation
of the human from transcendent embodiments, authorities, and heteronomies, and the human transformation
of nature by education and technical subjection. But
this ideal was turned down by an astonishing process of
self-defiance with subsequent dehumanization and the
loss of reason as a human principle. Nature conquered
reason in the process of production. The process became more and more the second nature of an incalculable character. Special mechanisms grew together and
became one vast mechanism which determines everyone's fate. The individual became an element in this
process through which one cannot look but which determines one's fate. Either it takes one into it, or it
pushes one out to the nothingness of unemployment, or

it draws one into its contradictions and destroys one in the slaughter of totalitarian war. The fate of modern humanity is in the process of economic production that humanity has created and that now has humanity in its hand for life or death. We call this stage "monopoly capitalism." Reason has been turned from a creative principle into a mere calculating means-end relation without a real meaning and end. Reason has become the inhuman principle of technical adequacy for a system without meaning. Instrumentalism and logical positivism express this very well.

The symptoms of dehumanization are seen in the mechanism of production, which makes people tools of the process by taking away the might of realizing oneself as a person; in this sense it destroys justice and love. This is expressed in external and internal symptoms. Instead of vocation (reserved for very few people: for instance, ministers), people are given "jobs" and prepared for them by an education of adjustment. Reason is reduced to cleverness in finding a higher place in this productive mechanism. This is supported by all the technical means of public communication encouraging humans to adapt.

The internal reaction is the fear of existence expressed by saying that it is better to be killed by bombs than to be unemployed. In the will to security, servitude is affirmed as better than freedom. In the feeling of loneliness, following a demonic power is thought better than remaining a lonely atom in a strange, nonhuman process. The feeling of emptiness considers it better to believe in some strong person or movement than to have permanent nihilism. All of this is an expression of the situation of production. Therefore, it will only be overcome with this situation and not with internal means of adaptation.

The modern world is disrupted by antinational upheavals. The revolt of life promises to overcome the fears nationalism evoked (even the Democrats have taken it up). Totalitarianism promises salvation. But since the totalitarian revolt is nationalistic itself, it cannot overcome the basic problem but only leads to even more fear.

The *Leviathan* of Hobbes was a prophecy of a wholly dominating state. Nobody knows how to escape it, even in the democracies which fight against its fascist form.

The Demands for the Peace

First there is a way peace should not be attempted. The declaration of the Conservative party in England on September 4, 1943, is an example. It demands the return of religious teaching in the schools, but as a means to a finite purpose—maintaining the state's present social order. It said, "There is a very real danger that the emptiness (lack of belief) may come to be occupied by a kind of emotional materialism, copied from the Russian original but lacking the historical roots which give the contemporary Russian materialism a spiritual factor." This shows all the problems together. Note the uneasiness about Russia, the use of religion as a means of preventing a social transformation, and calling this transformation materialism because it asks for the economic reasons for this emptiness for which the declaration gives no reason at all. The idea of the "opiate of the people" has never been more clearly expressed than in this statement. No teacher in religion should be admitted who does not understand that the teaching must "render unto Caesar the things that are Caesar's." This is similar to Lutheran conservatism, which has always abused this word to restrain religious criticism of politics. If this is the pattern of the future peace, it is lost before it starts. But the reactionary groups in this country are even more dangerous. Not needing the religious cover, they will perhaps use the expeditionary army to get rid not only of the Nazis but also of revolutionaries in Germany and Russia altogether, and also elements of the New Deal here. For this purpose they would need to use the bureaucratic mechanism of the New Deal without its social content and go to the American brand of state capitalism.

This can be prevented only by an alliance of British social movements, Russia, the central European underground, and New Deal trends here. All of this needs support from strong sections of the church. This is the alliance by which the peace must be won, if it can be won at all.

The best political structure to be reached by the next step is a liberalized state capitalism in which the chaotic insecurity of monopolism is excluded and the individual can participate actively in the process of production. Beyond this next step we cannot see. But if this self-destructive mechanism does not come to an end, the sacrifices of the present war may be as much in vain as those of the last war—perhaps not completely so but certainly in vain for us and for our children's generation.

Lecture III: The International Problem of a Just and Durable Peace

The international problem is secondary to the social problem if you accept the theory of structural necessity. But it is not simply dependent on economic structures; it is at the same time independent, because nations are still the vehicles of social realities. Therefore the solution of one is impossible without the other.

The Idea and the Reality of the World

The idea of the world equals the cosmos and it is equal to the concept of order. The concept of the cosmos is related to the idea of national order. The prophets discovered the idea of the world in the unity of all nations and moved from there to the unity of the created order. But historical elements predominate in the biblical conceptions. If God as the Lord is God related to the world and beyond the world, the world may fall away from God. The idea of the world expresses both the cosmos of evil and the world as the object of God's love. World history as an idea emerges with the prophets. It is involved in the idea of a God who can resist his nation without becoming lost.

The national imperialism of the ancient nations is based on the world structure of being itself. They attempt to extend to the limits what is considered potentially to be the world.

The Roman Empire is the presupposition of Christianity's ecumenical sense. It contained the will to center and it had the will to become central, even if not just. Augustine challenged the injustice of Roman imperialism and replaced the empire with the church. The revolt against the church's practical power released the autonomous nations and their sovereignty. The belief in an autonomous balance of power, or of nationalism controlled by a hidden law, reflected the Christian tradition of universal reason. But this never really worked because there were always hegemonic powers: Spain, France, England.

In our time the new concept of a world history is more than an idea. The technical superstructure is the uniting power. But its uniting power is felt in the sense of destruction all around the world. This new reality has brought about a new situation. Humanity faces the alternative of either self-destruction or self-realization. The old balance of power is at an end. The old sovereignty reflected the contingent development of the bourgeois society. The new search for union is a result of this monopolistic, imperialistic, chaotic situation of meaningless sovereignty.

Different types of imperialism have characterized the drive toward a world. Cultural imperialism has flowed from Macedonia, Greece, Rome, and France. Religious imperialism has come from the elected nation and then from the elected ones all over the world in the church. Power and religion were united in the German empire of the Middle Ages, Anglo-Saxon imperialism, and Spanish imperialism. Economic imperialism flowed from bourgeois society and only indirectly from the proletariat. But both were swallowed by national concentrations of power. Therefore it concluded in National Socialism and in universal transformation.

It is impossible to combine sovereignty with the world in the present situation. The present is against national resignation of sovereignty in military or economic terms.

However, if it should happen—and some say it will happen—how can national sovereignty be overcome? Three ways are under discussion. The World War makes some expect a world power as a central unity to which everybody contributes. Alternatively, bigger regions are necessary; the world could be organized as Europe, East Asia, Russia, the Americas, and the British Commonwealth. Or the Anglo-Saxon nations could represent the power center and be expected to administer the world in a way that is liberal toward the others.

The Just World Order

The fragmentary and ambiguous character of justice is extremely obvious. We know the need of the kairos: to transform the technical-nationalistic reality of the world into a political-spiritual reality. What are the presuppositions?

In the treatment of the conquered, what is just? The Germans are the aggressors and they will be the first conquered. They will be conquered because they were defeated by the groups in the Allied nations who favored National Socialism as long as it was the only power against the socialist movements and against Russia. Who is more guilty, the German people or those who helped deliver them as tools to the demonic? Beyond this, the negative attitude toward the German people contradicts the principle of self-realizing life and love. Germany has to be included in an embracing nation participating in the center of Europe. This policy is against the disarmament of the aggressor without an equally radical disarmament of every sovereign state. But is there any chance for justice? Will not the understandable revenge of the conquered nations create a national destruction before anything positive can happen? Is it not the situation of prophetic judgment that doom is unavoidable, whatever may happen? What am I to say in radio broadcasts to Germany? Church statements are helpful on this situation, but are they realistic?

How will we treat Russia? She carried the biggest burden of the war. Shall she participate in the occupation of Europe or shall she stay behind the Vistula, weakened by the Germans to such an extent that her aspirations and ideas cannot compete with those of the

Western countries? Or if she is attacked by Japan, will
her influence in Asia be finished?

What about the small nations? Is it just to reestablish
Luxembourg and all the others as independent states,
even if a plebiscite decides to do so? Could twenty
national sovereignties mean justice? The nations themselves are not as anxious for sovereignty as are the diplomatic representatives who want their privileges back.

On the Indian question: Is the ideology of India taking the burden of India upon herself more just than a
venturing out that gives her freedom and risks dangers
in order to avoid the betrayal of the ideal? But even if
the better method is used, does not a new nationalism
arise after it has just been overcome in Europe? What
is justice against Japan? Or for Java? Is the idea of a
nation not ridiculous here? Has not the modern history
of Asia just started?

There is also the question of the possibility of a European or a world federation. Is there a common spirit
that can carry this or that federation? Are there sociological strata able to make an international community?
Nothing can be accomplished on the basis of sovereign
nations. But where is the power to provide a center? If
the power is not there, must it not be accomplished in
the imperialistic way?

The solution of Anglo-Saxon dominance would mean
that America must lead. But is she willing and able to
give the centralizing power to a historical world? Could
America teach Europe? Or would she control Europe
and leave it alone? Would this be the just peace? And
how will America look? Will it be a social or a capitalistic America that dominates Europe, and could either
American development lead toward justice in Europe?

Considering the churches, the ecumenical movement is the foreshadowing of the world, if the lack of
unity talked about previously does not make it impossible. Besides this, the church is a part of the whole situation, bound to nations and social classes. Secularism is
still more powerful, and in any case the church is not
the political power that could carry the new world.
There were Allied leaders who prophesied the doom of
Christianity if the Allied nations were not victorious. If

this were true, Christianity deserves to be doomed, but the church has always been the underground center of the world historical process.

Everything is just which creates the world unity of love. But this may be impossible because the divine wrath is upon us. The prophecy of the end may be realized first. This is the tragic aspect of the situation. It must be faced as the prophets faced it. Beyond this lie grace and historical destiny for what is left.

So in the name of Christian principles and the prophetic tradition, I have argued the necessity of destroying the moralistic arrogance of the concept of a just and durable peace in a situation in which tragedy and possibly grace are the only categories that can be applied to the present disrupted world.

5

Power and Justice
in the Postwar World

The topic of power and justice in the postwar world is approached as an essay in applied theology. It presupposes philosophical theology and practical knowledge. The philosophical theology that analyzes the concepts of power and justice is intrinsic to my teaching field at Union Theological Seminary. The practical knowledge is derived from conversation with a group of friends consisting of German refugee scholars and some Americans. But I cannot claim any expertise in the fields of politics, economics, or foreign relations. The practical application of the philosophical concepts also reflects my work as a theologian within the religious socialist movement of Republican Germany, and so it reflects a definite perspective. The essay does not present a full picture of postwar reconstruction but shows the bearing of some theological concepts on the postwar situation.[1]

---

[1]The first paragraph has been rewritten from the unedited speech manuscript to present Tillich's ideas in the form of an essay. This essay, though very important for its presentation of the early form of his analysis of the concepts of love, power, and justice, contains many dated references from 1944. His passions for political unification and economic security in Europe are clear. The evolution of Europe in these directions is still shaky in 1990. His writing about forces moving toward conflict in a postwar settlement was of course in 1944 innocent of any knowledge of the threat of nuclear war. Perhaps the Western world did better in Europe than he anticipated, for despite the eclipsing of his socialist hopes and vocabulary, Europe has moved toward social security under mixed economic and political economies—EDITOR.

Power and Justice as Principles

Three assertions shall be made in this section, dealing with power and justice as theological principles: first, that power by its very definition implies justice; second, that justice by its very definition implies power; third, that both power and justice are implied in love as the highest concept by which the structure of being as being can be described.

Power Implies Justice

Theologians ordinarily have a certain distrust of the application of the term "power" in social ethics. They want to eliminate it entirely or they accept it sadly as an unavoidable evil. The same theologians, however, do not hesitate to pray to God, "the almighty and all powerful," thus making power a divine attribute and, even more, making it the fundamental attribute, that which never can be missed because it makes God God. But if power is the divine quality, there is no reason not to use it affirmatively for humanity and the world.

And certainly it would demand a complete closing of our eyes in the face of reality if we did not see the power structure of everything that is, that participates in being. This leads me to a philosophical statement. When I am asked to say in one word what being is, I like to answer, "The power to exist." Instead of "being," the most abstract of all possible concepts, we sometimes should say the "might of being," the potency of coming to existence and sustaining oneself in existence. If such a statement is made, it obviously implies a high ontological valuation of power, the highest that can be given to a concept; it is the first and basic description of being-itself. The philosophical concept of power is the basic attribute of being, as the theological concept of power is the basic attribute of God. And this is so, of course, not by chance, for God *is* being, not *a* being, but being-itself.

Every single thing and all more embracing structures of reality in nature, man, and society participate in this basic structure of being; they are all structures of power. They exercise the power of existence in every moment, providing time and space, substance and causality for themselves in a continuous interdependence with all other beings. If this power weakens or leaves them completely, their existence is endangered or finished. The power of being is the power of uniting the elements that belong to the structure of a thing— for instance, the cells and physiological processes in a living body; and it is, at the same time, the power of actualizing oneself within the power constellation of all the other beings that forms one's nearer or farther environment. So the power of every being is determined by these two factors of internal and external power: its power of being in unity with itself and its power of being in unity with the whole to which it belongs— ultimately, the universe.

One more word must be said about the character of this power of being. It is a dynamic power. It is a continuous activity, an attempt to push beyond the given limits or a necessity of falling below these limits, an oscillation between venturing courage and cautious self-restriction. This is the way in which the trees in a forest and the birds in a flock and the pupils in a class and the cells in a body and the nations on a continent are acting. This is life itself. But this is only one side. No being can push infinitely beyond its limits. Every being has its static structure, which makes it what it is. The tree is not a bird, and the fish is not a man, and the child is not an adult, and no being is God. The power of every being is that in pushing beyond itself it does not destroy its static basis, its essential structure, the root of its power, as, for instance, the German nation did twice in this century.

And now it is not difficult to show the ground of our first statement, that power by its very definition implies justice. *Justice is the order of powers according to their dynamic and static potentialities.* A just order is an order in which every part gets what it deserves according to the structure of power it represents: Stones, that they are used for buildings; plants, that they are planted and harvested; animals, that they are fought if dangerous, taken care of if useful, respected in their own power of being wherever we meet them; humans, that they are acknowledged as persons with infinite dignity because they are human and are individuals with infinite differences in their actual power of being.

No power can exist without a just order within itself and outside itself. A body that fails to balance the different parts and functions constituting it becomes sick and finally dies. This refers to a social body as much as to a biological and psychological body. An individual or a group that does not obtain justice within a larger unity according to its power of being is destroyed or destroys the whole by its reactions. A permanently unemployed person loses his own power of being because of the structural contradiction of this situation to his humanity, or in unity with others in the same situation, he destroys the social organism that deprives him of the actualization of basic human power, that of creative freedom. Even the worst tyranny needs a certain amount of justice, at least a silent acknowledgment by its subjects that obedience to the tyrant is better than death, that it makes life possible; this means that it provides a certain amount of justice. If this limit is trespassed, the tyrant is doomed. There is, of course, a very large amount of room for movement before the limit is reached. One of the most horrible visions is that of Huxley's *Brave New World,* in which the lower groups, by refined educational methods, are emasculated in their dynamic power of being to such a degree that they are not only not dissatisfied with their dehumanized situation, without any creative freedom; they are proud of it. Justice for them is complete mechanization, combined with security. We should be clear about the fact that the conscious or subconscious aim of fascism is just such a psychological state of the masses, to be produced and reproduced by the technical means of communication, managed by a monopolistic group. We have already gone part of the way in this direction. One of the trends for the postwar world is based on such a conception of justice for the masses. Even so, our basic statement is valid. There is no power without justice,

even if, in the light of our present standards, it is a very
poor justice. At least power must be felt as justice by
those subjected to it.

Justice Implies Power

Justice not only presupposes but implies power. The
very concept of justice cannot be carried through without the element of power. For justice is the principle of
order, and no order has existence without an ordering
power. In plants and animals and human bodies, the
ordering power is the centralization to which everything is subjected when it becomes an element of the
body. If it resists the power of centralization and the
general life-plan of the organism, it either will be
ejected or it will destroy the organism. In social groups
the centralizing and planning power can be a kind of
social common sense that is effective in all of its members and can reject or assimilate strange influences.
Among the modern civilized nations, the Anglo-Saxons
have developed this type of "power through conformism" more than other nations.

Justice in such a social structure is actualized more
smoothly than in nonconformistic nations. But it is not
carried through without power. Dissenting people of
all kinds in Great Britain have felt the power of this
commonsense conformism as strongly as the power of
tyrannical government in other countries. If the more
collectivistic society is based on a commonsense conformism, the chances for creative freedom will not be
much better than they would be in a society of a nonconformistic type with a strong bureaucratic power. In
any case, this smooth conformism makes the Anglo-
Saxon philosophers often forget not only that social conformism can be a very suppressing power but also that
this conformity was created by a tremendous pressure
of internal and external powers: wars of conquest, wars
of revolution, and social oppression.

Justice, although implied in power, is at the same
time the fruit of a successful use of power. The League
of Nations could not produce even a small amount of
international justice because it could not use power.

The labor movements have achieved only as much social justice as they could reach by the threat or the application of power. The justice achieved in the United States could be maintained only by the power of the victorious states in the Civil War. This has happened in former centuries in all great nations. No international justice will be achieved without the superior power of the victorious nations bringing about a system of international justice based on a centralized world power, but certainly not on a cleverly calculated balance of power. Of course, there is always a balance of powers within a larger unity, as for instance in a biological and social organism. But a balance that is not effective *within* a unity is the declaration that there is no justice in this system, but only balanced injustice.

Justice and Power Presuppose a Common Principle

Justice implies power as power implies justice. But they are not the same, and they may be detached from each other and become destructive and self-destructive at the same time. Power is always represented by a central organ that stands for the whole as well as for itself. A basic distortion is rooted in this ambiguous position of all representatives of power. They trespass their essential and genuine power (which has made them the bearers of the power of the whole) by using their representative power for themselves. No ruling class and no ruling nation has ever escaped the tragic implications of this tendency, and none ever will. In doing so, it destroys the justice it originally embodied and the basis of its own power. In order to meet this tendency, the division of power, checks and balances, and democratic procedures have been introduced. Justice was supposed to restrict power by these methods, and in many ways it did. But it did something else also: Justice detached from power became more and more abstract, formal, and equalitarian in a technical sense, and the representative power, in the same measure, became more and more undermined and unable to act for the establishment of real justice. This had a third consequence: Since there is no empty space in the realm of power, other powers, neither central nor representative—and this means not responsible—take the place of the emptied representative powers; for instance, the leaders of the great monopolies. So it was in the German Republic and in France; it is also the most serious danger for the future of this country—and this means today—for its ability to direct the destiny of humanity.

The tension between justice and power leads to the quest for a uniting principle above both arbitrary power and formal justice. This principle is love. Speaking of love in this fundamental sense I do not mean the human affections of Eros or sympathy. I also do not mean the *agape* of which the New Testament speaks. All these meanings of love are rooted in the love-structure of being-itself. Being is a continuous process of separating individualization and reuniting communion. The more separation, that is, independent selfhood or self-centeredness, the greater the power of reunion, that is, of love. Love in its highest form accepts the separation of self, and self overcomes it only by a mutual participation of one life in the other life, creating a more powerful life by communion.

Applying this principle of love to the relation of power and justice, we must say: Justice is what creates communion. And the power that unites these independent beings is justified because it fulfills the structure of being-itself. This implies two negative statements: Nothing is just only because it agrees with an abstract form of justice. And no power is justified that extinguishes independence to create union.

From these positive and negative statements follows the criterion for postwar reconstruction. Every solution in which power and justice are separated is wrong. But, of course, whether a concrete solution is a union of power and justice, in which more justice creates more power and vice versa, is a matter of a venturing decision that may be tragically false. Nevertheless, we must risk it and avoid in every decision the spirit of legalism, namely the abstract application of the principle of justice, as much as the spirit of imperialism, namely the application of power for the sake of power.

The Structure of Power and the Possibilities of Justice in the Postwar World

Power is always given. It can increase, but it cannot be produced since only power could produce power. You can increase the power of an animal but you cannot make a human of it. You can increase the power of a small nation but you cannot make a big nation of it. There are preestablished conditions in nature and history in the frame of which power and justice must work. It is a self-betrayal if we demand equal rights for small and big nations. Even if they have formal equality, the difference in power will reduce the formal equality to insignificance.

The Structure of Power After the War

The present war will decide for a long time the question of which powers will be world powers, that is, powers which by their very existence participate in every essential decision about the structure of the coming world. Germany and Japan will be excluded for a long time, and perhaps forever, from being world powers. The immediate meaning of this war is that these two competitors are defeated in their claim for world power. Three powers remain with a substantial claim to control the destiny of mankind: America, Great Britain, Russia. It is only a matter of political politeness toward China to speak of the Big Four. In reality, China is neither a centralized power nor a world power in any conceivable sense of the word.

In the constellation of the Big Three, there will be a large amount of economic competition between America and Great Britain, and a part of the dominions will incline more toward the United States than to England. But these difficulties do not seem insuperable. This situation differs from that between the Anglo-Saxons and Russia. Here two systems of life and thought clash with each other. And all the nice statements that the two systems can live peacefully beside each other are meaningless if we consider that both of them will participate in decisions about Europe and Asia. It is not a pessimistic exaggeration but a simple statement of fact when I say that the diplomatic preparation for the next war has already started. It may be postponed by clever diplomatic compromises, but ultimately it will happen, because the only way of preventing it is made nearly, although not entirely, impossible by the economic power structure. This is the second point in the description of the given structure of power: The armies that liberate the European nations, including Germany, from Nazism are poised to maintain the social situation out of which Nazism has grown, namely monopoly capitalism in a stage of development in which it is unable to satisfy the needs of humanity and to protect the masses from the most destructive form of economic insecurity. The official policy of the United Nations is an economic status-quo policy, represented by the American State Department and most of the governments in exile. This means that the European masses will be attracted by the Russian solution and that the Anglo-Saxons will have to maintain a strong military force in Europe in order to keep down social revolutions, whether they are tried with or without Russian help. This is another, and I think the most fundamental, feature in the power structure of the postwar world. The fact that British people, especially the soldiers, are passionately against the economic status-quo policy of the present cabinet does not count very much, considering the inclination of the dominions to the American system and the tremendous prestige of the Prime Minister. It is interesting to see how quickly the promises of the Atlantic Charter have disappeared from public discussion and are seriously mentioned only by people such as Vice President Wallace, who knows about the interdependence of social and political problems, but who does not have even the American labor movement on his side.

There is a third realm in which the power structure of the postwar world is already visible: the realm of national politics. In all countries, authoritarian trends of a more or less antidemocratic character are developing. The need for planning on the ruins of continents makes this imperative. Everything depends on the power groups who will do the planning, for instance, a planning as envisaged in the two Beveridge Plans. The picture as it is taking shape looks like a combination of state- and big-business bureaucracies, supported in some European countries by reactionary forces such as the Catholic hierarchy, supported in other countries, as in the United States, by half-fascist antilabor groups. The other possibility is, of course, social revolution or simple subjection to Russia, which would mean the elimination of big business and the establishment of an almighty state bureaucracy. Between these possibilities, nineteenth-century liberal democracy has no chance at all in Europe and Asia and will be undermined in this country to the extent to which Big Business (which fights the New Deal bureaucracy) establishes a bureaucracy of its own, not to return to the Old Deal but to replace an emasculated New Deal with a streamlined, centralized "Newest Deal." This is, at least, the idea of the more enlightened and far-seeing managers of the great enterprises.

This is the power situation in the world after the war: the Big Three and their imperialistic and ideological tensions; the economic status-quo forces in America and Europe; the inescapable trend toward bureaucratic centralization and authoritarianism. How much justice can be expected and fought for under these conditions? Before trying to address this question, I want to state once more as clearly as possible the criterion for any possible answer, derived from the systematic interpretation of power and justice. It is meaningless to demand structures of justice not implied in the described structures of power, at least as possibilities. It is, for instance, meaningless to demand a continental European federation, an idea which was very near to my heart and to which I gave literary expression in an early stage of the war. The Big Three will by no means admit the creation of a fourth big power in terms of a new world power: "Europe." Most of the European nations concerned have already declared that under no circumstances would they accept a federation with seventy million Germans in it. The idea of a political European federation is out, even if it were in the line of justice. This justice is abstract, not real justice; it lacks the power of creating community. It fails to fulfill the demand of love, in which power and justice are united.

There is another type of abstract justice that must be excluded, not because it is impossible from the point of view of power but from the point of view of the purpose of *just* power to create community. I give the question of reparations as an example. The obligation to return what one has taken by force seems to be especially just. But how does this look in reality under the conditions of the postwar ruin of Europe and especially of Germany? The Jews are certainly justified in demanding reparations. But how shall this be done in cities like Cologne and Hamburg, which are a total loss for everybody? Shall the Germans pay money for them to foreign countries? But most of these foreign countries demand at least the same reparations for themselves. Shall they give it to the German Jews? Beyond this: Money transfer with devalued money is impossible. The transfer of goods is possible only so long as it is not competitive in the markets of the countries which are paid. Compulsory labor in foreign countries may be a partial solution as long as there is a labor shortage in the victorious countries, but it certainly will not serve the reparation of Jewish property or any other's individual property. It will, in fact, only serve the reconstruction of European Russia for her defense against the attack she expects from the Allied powers. All these considerations show that such a simple demand of formal justice has very little to do with real justice, namely the creation of communion, the establishment of higher unities of power and justice.

These two examples, the European Federation and reparations, especially with respect to the Jews, show the injustice of formal justice.

Possibilities of Justice Within the Postwar Structure of Power

But these examples do not show that justice in another sense, namely in the sense of the establishment of communion, is impossible. It is now my last task to give some examples which, on the one hand, illuminate the principles developed before, and, on the other hand, give some indications about the way in which I believe a solution must be sought that unites power and justice.

While the description of the situation of power necessarily started with the three world powers that will exist after the war, the description of the possibilities of justice must start with the economic situation of the European masses, the real victims of the two world wars and the real key to the future. Without the injustices of later capitalism, toward the proletariat as much as toward the lower middle classes, the twentieth century would not have become the century of the great antibourgeois revolutions. Fascism and Nazism belong in this line. Without the economic, social, and spiritual disintegration of the nineteenth-century social systems, no dictator could have arisen. The dictators were considered to be the creators of a new social justice, in spite of all their sins against formal justice. No organization of the postwar world can be called just, even with all the restrictions mentioned before, which does not fulfill the demand for security. For "security" is the catchword of the twentieth-century revolution in the midst of which we are living.

Social justice for the European masses is necessary and not entirely impossible from the point of view of power. The European masses, especially in Central Europe, are broader than the proletariat. Nazism, combined with the war needs, has completely destroyed the lower middle classes. They have become proletarian masses, in the technical sense that they have no property except their working power. If they are prevented from selling it, they will be the center of all kinds of desperate upheavals and revolutions. The world will not have one quiet moment without European social security after the Allied occupation is finished.

Such a plan demands the organization of European big industry and agriculture, including transportation and large-scale trade, in such a way that the ruinous competitive production in small, national, self-exclusive units is overcome. A reasonable scheme of division of labor for the sake of full employment and a rising standard of living must be introduced. This super-cartel or European investment bank would be dependent on a board in which representatives of governments and of private property decide together. Such a scheme is a technical possibility in economic terms. It is a demand of justice in social terms. And it is the only conceivable way to justice in international terms.

For it would produce a pacified Europe. If the European people are subjected to an organization that guarantees security and a rising standard of life, their revolutionary tendencies would cease and with them their trend toward Russia. As I heard an outstanding French Protestant leader say, "We can overcome the threat of the Russification of Europe only when we give the European masses what the Russian way would give them: social security."

On the other hand, Russia would not feel threatened by a Europe that has overcome within itself the necessary aggressiveness of a disintegrating monopoly capitalism, the soil on which fascist tendencies necessarily grow. It is also this way alone that can solve the otherwise insoluble problems of the boundary lines between the European nations. The only, and the only *just*, solution is that the boundaries become insignificant. Nobody ever was able to imagine a just solution of the territorial claims of the Balkans. But the situation will become even more serious when Germany is dismembered. The small nations say that they are not willing to continue living under the threat of seventy million Germans united in *one* state. But if Germany is divided into three sovereign nations, the eastern part in the Russian sphere of influence, the western in the British, and the southern in the American sphere of influence, then the greatest irredenta in world history will be created.

But if the same scheme is combined with a European security plan by which economic frontiers are abolished, the framework means an administrative division without fundamental importance for the life of the individual citizen. If the masses realize that they can live and that there is hope for their future—something they had entirely lost under the system of social insecurity of disintegrating capitalism, no nationalistic propaganda will appeal to them. Moreover, there will be no nationalistic education in the old sense, since the ruling classes would not need to use nationalism to divert the masses from their misery. It will not be necessary to give them war work, as in the monopolistic stage of capitalism, in which productive work cannot be created for a large part of the population. Consequently, aggressive nationalism that has brought such an incredible amount of misery will disappear since it is not reproduced again and again as a political weapon.

There are two more problems implied in the power structure of the postwar world that can be solved in the direction of justice, if the basic social justice is established. The first is the problem of centralized authority. Centralization always has technical and psychological disadvantages. But those disadvantages are by far outbalanced if the centralization gives social security. This, of course, cannot appear in a system determined by profit or fascism. In a socially secure system, however, even if it is distinctly authoritarian, as indeed it *has* to be, the interplay between repression from above and aggression from below *can* be reduced to a minimum. Power and justice *can* be united. They *can* be united in still another respect: in the educational realm. Much discussion goes on about the education of the Axis countries. I want to emphasize as strongly as possible that no educational enterprise performed by the Allied victors has any meaning if it is not based in an interpretation of a social reality that is convincing by itself. The teaching of democratic principles and the reestablishment of a system of social insecurity are contradictory tasks. The European masses will reject such teaching with utter cynicism if it is not accompanied by the establishment of a better "new order" than the one Hitler promised them.

There *is* an inroad for justice in the power jungle of the postwar situation. The name of this inroad is "European social security." But after having painted this

somewhat bright picture of a way to justice (the only
one I can see), I must now raise the power question
once more. At this moment the picture becomes
gloomy and dark. I do not point to the technical possibilities of my solution. They are, according to advanced
economic thought, beyond doubt. Humanity has developed a productive power that surpasses all imagination,
not only of the fairy tales of the past but also of ourselves who have seen so much of it. The greatest injustice would be to bury these possibilities under a system
that serves the power of the few and not the human-
ized existence of the many. But this is the threat implied in the present structure of power. Since the
United States will emerge as the greatest power after
the war, this threat should be the highest concern of
every responsible American.

Foreign policy is to a great extent a function of the
political situation at home. Which forces are willing to
support a European social security plan? The decisive
authority has to be the "European Council," that is, the
board through which the Big Three administer the
European reorganization. Which domestic American
and British forces will influence this council? What role
will America play in it? Perhaps a secondary one, supporting Great Britain more than acting herself. But if
a European economic reconstruction and the unification of its productive power for the sake of social security and a rising standard of living are intended, these
cannot be achieved without the productive powers of
this country. But are the ruling economic forces ready
to give this support to such a purpose? Or will each of
these forces buy out of the European bankruptcy what
it can catch and use it for the increase of world economic power instead of for some economic justice in
Europe? Will the American government be strong
enough against these groups: for instance, the American bankers whose report produced a general shaking
of the heads even among the British Tories? Will it be
said of them as it was said of the French refugees when
they returned after the Revolution: "They have
learned nothing and forgotten nothing"?

One more example in this connection: the question

of German industry or what is left of it. Shall it be
dismantled and sent to Russia? This would mean that
twenty million Germans must be exported as slave
workers and can never return; it also means that the
greatest productive power of Europe will be destroyed
and the standard of living of all European countries will
go down tremendously. On the other hand, if German
industry is rebuilt, who can supervise it to prevent it
from the preparation of a new war? The only answer is
this: There shall not be a German industry but there
shall be a European industry *in* Germany as well as in
all other countries to serve the masses of the European
peoples.

What are the signs pointing in this or that direction?
They are not encouraging. I leave it to those who know
more than I about politics in this country to judge in
which direction the events in Congress point. But I
want to mention two events that seem to indicate very
clearly that power and justice will *not* go together in
the postwar world. The one is the choice made by the
invasion armies in Africa, Italy, and France with respect to the national groups with whom they are dealing. In all cases it is the representatives of the vested
interests and, even more, of the most reactionary type
of the vested interests that they have chosen. The other
sign is the response to this policy: the Alliance of Underground France under the leadership of de Gaulle, and
the "Free German Committee" in Russia. This is the
logical consequence of a policy of the Anglo-Saxons
which gives the European antifascist masses no hope
for an era of social justice at all.

The role of the church in the union of power and
justice is implicit in that the tension between power
and justice can only be solved by the principle of love
and the creation of communion in an ever-increasing
space. The church by its very foundation is beyond the
principle of mere power as much as beyond the principle of formal justice. It is, nevertheless, always in a
double danger: It may either support given powers
without preaching in a strong way the prophetic message of justice (this is the danger of all established
churches), or it may preach an abstract gospel of justice

behind which no power stands and which, therefore, is not only ineffective but gives comfort to the forces of injustice, which are not really hit by such a message. This is the danger of the sectarian and humanistic movements in the church.

The postwar world needs both elements. It needs a new marriage of power and justice in the unity of love.

6

A Program
for a Democratic Germany

Only through cooperation between the Western powers and Russia will it be possible to achieve the reconstruction of Europe which must follow the necessary and certain defeat of Hitler Germany. This has been borne out clearly by the military and political course of the war. Any kind of unilateral settlement in Europe imposed by the East or the West would lay the foundations of new worldwide conflicts. With this view in common, a number of persons belonging to various professions, groups, and affiliations have united to make known their stand on the question of the future of Germany within the framework of a solution of the European problem. All of the signers are natives of Germany and have fought against Nazism from the beginning. For all their experience in non-German countries, whether or not they have become citizens, has shown them new and broader horizons of political thinking.

We cannot claim to have a formal mandate from people now inside Germany. We believe, however, that we typify some of the forces and tendencies which will be vitally needed in the creation of a new Germany within the framework of a free world. We therefore feel that it is our duty in the interest of the United States and the United Nations to express our conviction about the future of Germany at a time when the German people cannot speak for themselves. We do this in full independence and according to the democratic practice of the United States.

I

The solution of the German problem is a part of the solution of the European problem. The just claims of all the nations of Europe for reconstruction and for security must be met. In reorganizing Europe and in solving the German problem, conditions must be created which will forestall a third world war. It is inevitable that the German people will have to bear the consequences of the war into which Hitler has driven them. It is, however, self-evident that a lasting solution of the European question is only possible if there is a creative solution of the German question.

The prerequisite for any such solution is the defeat of Nazism, the destruction of those who brought Nazism to power, and the obliteration of its spirit in Germany and throughout the world. This will be accomplished in the battle for the liberation of Europe, by the coming liquidation of the Nazis, by the Germans themselves, and in the prosecution of the war criminals. But in addition, those groups which were the bulwarks of German imperialism and which were responsible for the delivery of power into the hands of the Nazis must be deprived of their political, social, and economic power. This applies particularly to the large landholders, the big industrialists, and the military caste whose political concepts and influence have had repeatedly a disastrous effect on German history. If, therefore, the German people will decide to dissolve large landholdings, to control heavy industry, to eliminate militarism, and to remove those civil servants, judges, and teachers beholden to these groups, they ought not to be impeded from the outside.

A disarmed Germany, together with the rest of the nations of Europe, must be fitted into the framework of a system of international security. It is taken for granted that Germany must return all conquered territory and that she must make good the damages she has caused to the limit of her ability. But it must not be forgotten that the first victims of National Socialism were large numbers of Germans who dared to oppose Hitler. The majority of the Germans did not want war. The opposition of Germans against Hitlerism is now forcing the Nazis even more to augment their terror organization and to maintain strong military units of occupation inside Germany. Policies leading to an enslavement of the German people and their pauperization must therefore be regarded as unwise and unjust. It should, furthermore, not be overlooked that to abandon the principles of the Atlantic Charter in *one* decisive case, means to abandon them in general.

It would be disastrous for the future of Europe if Germany were to be dismembered and split up economically and politically. This would create fertile soil for new pan-Germanist movements. It would prevent Germany from assuming responsibilities for the molding of her future and shift this heavy burden to other nations. It would create an irredentism which might well become the greatest such movement of all times. Useful energies of the victorious nations would be consumed in the permanent task of suppressing this irredenta.

II

It is essential for the economic future of Europe and the world that Germany's productive power be conserved. If it were destroyed, the economic conditions would become hopelessly depressed in all countries of Europe, and trade between Europe and other continents would be reduced largely. Moreover, millions of Germans would become permanently unemployed and condemned to an involuntary parasitic existence. Thus a constant source of unrest would arise in the very center of Europe.

Germany's productive strength should be integrated in an international system of production and consumption. Such a system would make possible the economic cooperation of the European peoples and would lessen the significance of political boundaries. Only in this way can Germany fulfill her obligations and make material reparations on a large scale, and only thus can Germany, with the rest of Europe, be protected against the threat of economic chaos. Germany's economic hegem-

ony and the danger of a rearming of Germany would
be eliminated.

III

If Germany is to develop a democracy, it is necessary
that the military and civil representatives of the United
Nations give political leeway from the beginning to
those who might best be able to create a new democracy. Moreover, it is necessary that all who shared in the
responsibility for the rise of Nazism, should be excluded, even if it would be expedient to deal with them.
On the other hand, all those must be considered who
resisted Nazism: for instance, the presently nameless
men and women now in the Gestapo prisons and the
concentration camps, trade unionists and workers of
the labor movement, those who resisted in the
churches and in the intellectual circles, in the middle
class, in the cities and in the country, and other quali-
fied individuals. The German democracy of the future
will depend on all those people. With their help, prepa-
rations must be made for the inauguration of an independent German government. Guarantees for the
establishment of the basic civil rights and liberties of
the people must be given without delay. Racial laws
must be abolished immediately. Religious and intellectual liberties must be restored. Freedom of the press, of
assembly, and of organization must be reestablished.
No obstacles should be placed in the way of the rebuild-
ing of a labor movement. The institutions set up by the
Nazis must be removed. Social and democratic institutions which the Nazis abolished must be recreated.

An attempt of the German people to stamp out Nazism root and branch, through a mass movement, and
to prepare the ground for democracy should be welcomed by the United Nations and should not be prevented or impeded under any circumstances. Only if
the German people free themselves from National Socialism through such an act of their own, will they be
entirely free. The victory of the United Nations will
break the external hold of Nazis over the German people. But only the German people can free themselves

spiritually. For this reason the German people should be given a peace which is constructive and gives them hope for the future, in spite of all burdens it must impose. Only this will enable Germany to develop and maintain a government of the people, by the people, and for the people.

IV

The education of the German people in democracy must spring from their own historical experience. There are signs that such a development is already under way. They are to be found in the old generation which was never entirely taken in by Nazism. They are to be found even among those who have been educated under the Nazi system. They are found to a lesser degree in the generation that brought Nazism to power and which is now bled white on the field of battle. Even in this generation, however, resistance is not lacking.

In connection with this education of the German people through the historical events, German youth must be educated by German democrats who have grasped the meaning of these events. Education by foreigners is psychologically impossible. It is, however, desirable to reestablish quickly and on a large scale cultural and scientific exchange between Germany and other countries. Facilities essential to intellectual life, such as universities, schools, textbooks, public libraries, theaters, movies, must be freed of all taints of Nazism. The German people must again be given the freedom to express and to develop their spiritual and cultural forces.

It must be emphasized most vigorously that no education is worthwhile whose principles are belied by the social conditions. Education for democracy without an attempt to actuate democracy will only create resistance and cynicism. The prerequisite for any successful education of the German people, and especially of the German youth to democracy and international cooperation, is a society which guarantees to all groups social security and the opportunity to lead a purposeful life.

The undersigned are convinced that it is impossible

to base the reconstruction of Europe on the enslavement of the German people. A new democratic Germany must be protected against the forces of reaction within and without. This need will be urgent from the moment hostilities cease. German democracy, permanently secured, will prove to be Germany's main contribution to the peace of Europe and the world.

7

The World Situation

I: The Meaning of "World Situation"

To speak of a "world situation" is no longer, as it was even during the nineteenth century, a matter of daring anticipation or utopian vision. Two world wars within a quarter century reveal that "world" as a historical reality has come into being.

"World" in the historical sense connotes such an interrelation of all political groups constituting mankind that events occurring in one section have direct repercussions upon all other sections. "World" in this sense, anticipated by a steady increase in worldwide communication and traffic, by world economic and political relationships, has existed since the First World War. The process advanced with accelerating speed before and during the Second World War.

To be sure, such a "world" exists only in the formal sense of the universal interdependence of all nations. As yet there is no unity of spirit, of culture, of organization, of purpose. Moreover, even the formal unity of the world is more apparent in the West than in the East, and the analysis which follows is necessarily mainly from the perspective of the Occident. Nevertheless, the forces which are transforming civilization are dominant not only in Europe and the Americas. They have penetrated from the West to the East, and not conversely, and have drawn Asia and Africa and Australasia also within a single revolutionary vortex. Therefore, it is not only possible but necessary to speak of a "world situation," to seek to discover the inner logic and meaning of that situation, and to ask what message Christianity has to offer it.

II: General Character of the Present World Situation

The present world situation is the outcome—directly in the West and indirectly elsewhere—of the rise, the triumph, and the crisis of what we may term "bourgeois society." This development has occurred in three distinguishable though overlapping phases. In the first, the new society struggled to establish itself over the remnants of a disintegrating feudal society—the period of bourgeois revolutions. In the second, mainly through the creation of a world mechanism of production and exchange, the new society came to triumphant power—the period of the victorious bourgeoisie. In the third, mankind struggles to regain control over the self-destructive forces loosed by a regnant industrial society—the present crisis in civilization. The disintegration and transformation of bourgeois society are at the dynamic center of the present world situation.

The Period of Bourgeois Revolutions

The first period was marked by great political, economic, and cultural revolutions in Western Europe and America. Feudalism and absolutism, both religious and political, were crushed. The bourgeois way of life became the determining though not the only influential factor in Western civilization.

The guiding principle of this revolutionary period was belief in reason. Reason did not mean the process of reasoning, but the power of truth and justice embodied in man as man. Man controlling nature and society was the ideal born in the humanistic theory of the Renaissance, ripened under the patronage of enlightened authoritarianism and brought to fulfillment through the bourgeois revolutions. Reason was the very principle of humanity which gives man dignity and liberates him from the slaveries of religious and political absolutisms. It is much more akin to the divine logos of the Stoics than to the manipulation of technical skills which won such triumphs in the second period of bourgeois society. The adoration of "Reason" as goddess in the French Revolution was a characteristic expression. The acknowledgment of every man as a rational being, capable of autonomy in his religious as well as his secular life, was the basis of the victorious struggle against the repressions of feudalism and every form of authoritarianism and tyranny.

In this struggle, out of which the modern world was born, one presupposition was always present, sometimes avowed, sometimes tacit. It was the belief that the liberation of reason in every person would lead to the realization of a universal humanity and to a system of harmony between individuals and society. Reason in each individual would be discovered to be in harmony with reason in every other individual. This principle of automatic harmony found expression in every realm of life. In the economic realm, it was believed that the welfare of all would be best served by the unrestrained pursuit by each individual of his own economic interests; the common good would be safeguarded by the "laws of the market" and their automatic functioning; this was the root principle of the economy of laissez-faire. In the political realm, it was supposed that the political judgment of each citizen would lead automatically to right political decisions by a majority of citizens; community of interest would assure sound democratic procedures. In the international realm, the play of interest among the nations would result in a comparatively stable balance of power between sovereign states. In the sphere of education, the essential rationality of human nature would produce, through free self-expression by each individual, a harmonious community. In religion, personal interpretation of the Bible and individual religious experience would follow a sufficiently uniform course among all believers to assure moral and spiritual conformity and to create and maintain a religious community of individual worshippers, the church. Finally, this all-controlling idea found philosophic expression in various doctrines of preestablished harmony, those of Leibnitz, Descartes, and their schools. The individual monad is a microcosm of the world. Ripening according to its own inner laws of logic, it develops in preestablished harmony with the whole of being.

This was the creed of the revolutionary movement in virtually all its intellectual and political leaders. Reality seemed to confirm it. Elements of automatic harmony could be discovered in every realm. The liberation of individual reason in economics and religion, in politics and education, did not bring on the disruptive consequences forecast by traditionalists and reactionaries. On the contrary, tremendous creativity was set free without the destruction of sufficient conformity to maintain national and religious communities. The enthusiastic belief in reason was vindicated by the prodigious achievements of mathematical science in the seventeenth century, by the development of autonomous national states after the disruptions of the Wars of Religion, by the establishment of natural laws in social and personal ethics. The law of harmony appeared to express the nature of reality. In the power of this belief, the new society overcame the resistance of feudalism and absolutism. In spite of all reactionary opposition, the nineteenth century may be regarded as the period of the victorious bourgeoisie.

The Period of the Victorious Bourgeoisie

Reason was supposed to control nature, in man and beyond man, because nature and reason were held to be in essential harmony. But in the measure in which the bourgeois revolution succeeded, the revolutionary impetus disappeared, and the character of reason as the guiding principle was transformed. The new ruling class could and did compromise with the remnants of feudalism and absolutism. They sacrificed reason as the principle of truth and justice, and employed it mainly as a tool in the service of the technical society they were bent upon perfecting. "Technical reason" became the instrument of a new system of production and exchange.

Technical reason provides means for ends but offers no guidance in the determination of ends. Reason in

the first period had been concerned with ends beyond
the existing order. Technical reason became concerned
with means to stabilize the existing order. Revolutionary reason had been conservative with respect to
means but "utopian" with respect to ends. Technical
reason is conservative with respect to ends and revolutionary with respect to means. It can be used for any
purposes dictated by the will, including those which
deny reason in the sense of truth and justice. The transformation of revolutionary reason into technical reason
was the decisive feature of the transition from the first
to the second period of modern society.

This displacement of revolutionary reason by technical reason was accompanied by far-reaching changes in
the structure of human society. Man became increasingly able to control physical nature. Through the tools
placed at his disposal by technical reason, he created a
worldwide mechanism of large-scale production and
competitive economy which began to take shape as a
kind of "second nature," a Frankenstein, above physical nature and subjecting man to itself. While he was
increasingly able to control and manipulate physical
nature, man became less and less able to control this
"second nature." He was swallowed up by his own creation. Step by step the whole of human life was subor-
dinated to the demands of the new worldwide
economy. Men became units of working power. The
profit of the few and the poverty of the many were
driving forces of the system. Hidden and irresponsible
powers controlled some parts of it, but no one the
whole. The movements of the mechanism of production and consumption were irrational and incalculable.
So it became for the masses a dark and incomprehensi-
ble fate, determining their destiny, lifting them today
to a higher standard of life than they had ever before
known, throwing them down tomorrow into utter misery and the abyss of chronic unemployment. The decisive feature of the period of the victorious bourgeoisie
is the loss of control by human reason over man's historical existence. This situation became manifest in the
two world wars and their psychological and sociological
consequences. The self-destruction of bourgeois society

and its elaborate scheme of automatic harmony is the characteristic of the present period of transition.

The Present Crisis in Civilization

Today the world stands in the third phase of modern history, though in varying degrees in different countries and continents. It has come to fullest expression in the industrial nations of continental Europe. In Anglo-Saxon lands, it has thus far achieved a fairly successful maintenance of the main features of the second period. In Russia and parts of Asia, it has come to power before the second stage had fully developed. These differences must be borne in mind. Their neglect would falsify the analysis and might lead to practical proposals which would be foredoomed to frustration. Nevertheless, it is possible to discern common structural trends which characterize contemporary world society in its various types. The dynamics of bourgeois society which have precipitated the present world situation have been dominant not only in the industrial nations of the European continent with their unbalanced economies, but likewise in Britain, America, and some smaller European countries with their comparatively stable situations, and also in Russia and the East, where resentment against the intrusion of dominating Western exploitation has led to a leap from the first to the third stage of modern social development, from a feudal and authoritarian society to a totalitarian order.

In the third period which determines our world situation, the foundation of bourgeois society has broken down; namely, the conviction of automatic harmony between individual interest and the general interest. It has become obvious that the principle was true only to a limited degree and under especially favorable circumstances. Its validity was dependent upon certain conditions—the continuing power of traditional values and institutions strong enough to counteract the disruptive consequences of the principle; the increasing strength of a liberal economy powerful enough to counteract the inner contradictions of the system through intensive and extensive expansion; the vestigial hold of feudal and absolutistic remnants powerful enough to allay the transmutation of all social life into a market system. When these retarding and disguising factors disappeared, the principle of automatic harmony was revealed in all its patent insufficiency. Attempts to replace it by a planned economy began. "Rationalization" was invoked as a method of control over the "second nature."

Totalitarianism was the first step in this direction. One expression is the fascist systems. They could achieve partial success because they understood the breakdown of the principle of automatic harmony and satisfied the demand for a planned organization of the life of the masses. In certain important respects, the fascist systems mark an advance beyond bourgeois society. They have provided minimum security for all. They have reintroduced unassailable authorities and commanding obligations. For these purposes they have employed technical reason in the most effective manner. But the fascist systems could not succeed ultimately because their basis was national, and thus they increased the disruption of mankind instead of uniting it according to the principle of reason. They destroyed any remnant of revolutionary reason and replaced it by an irrational will to power. Absolutism returned, but without the social, cultural, and religious traditions which furnished solid foundations for the earlier absolute systems.

The other radical expression of the trend toward a planned society is the Soviet system. It could succeed for the same reasons which brought partial success to the fascist systems. And it achieved an even greater security for the masses. Moreover, it has retained, at least in principle, revolutionary reason as an ultimate critical principle. But it also was a return to absolutism without the traditional foundations. It has come under the control of a bureaucracy which is inclined to replace revolutionary reason by technical reason after the pattern of the second phase of bourgeois society. Freedom for the individual is as completely lost as under the fascist systems.

Both systems are reactions against the bourgeois faith

in automatic harmony. Both are ambiguous: on the one
hand, they attempt to bring the incalculable mechanism of world economy back under the control of man;
on the other hand, they aggravate the self-destructive
forces generated by the second stage of bourgeois society. Both seek to elevate technical reason to "planning
reason"—the characteristic feature of the third period
and the determining principle of our present world
situation.

The logic of bourgeois society in its struggle for sur-
vival is expressed in the development of reason from
"revolutionary reason" through "technical reason" to
"planning reason." This development must be held
clearly in mind in every analysis of the present situation, in every question and answer regarding the future. This development cannot be reversed. We cannot
return to a half-feudal absolutism. Neither the spiritual
nor the economic conditions for such a return are present. We cannot return to the principle of automatic
harmony epitomized in laissez-faire liberalism in economics. The political and social conditions for reestab-
lishing the status quo have been destroyed by the
present world catastrophe. And faith in automatic harmony cannot be reestablished among the masses for
whom it has meant oscillation between war, boom, depression, and war renewed through thirty years. We
must go forward under the direction of planning reason
toward an organization of society which avoids both
totalitarian absolutism and liberal individualism. This is
not an easy course to define or to follow. Repelled by
the inhuman brutalities of totalitarian planning, we are
tempted to seek a return to a more or less concealed
laissez-faire solution. Or, disillusioned by the catastrophic discredit of the philosophy of automatic harmony, we incline toward some kind of absolutism. Our
task is to find a way between and beyond these extremes.

A biblical symbol may aid us in this attempt. When
Hobbes developed his theory of the absolute state, he
had recourse to the figure of Leviathan, the all-embracing portent which, in the interests of the state, swallows
all elements of independent existence, political and ec-

onomic, cultural and religious. Struggle against the Leviathan of late-medieval authoritarianism was the genius of the bourgeois revolutions. But the revolutionaries did not foresee that Leviathan was able to assume another face, not less formidable though disguised behind the mask of liberalism: the all-embracing mechanism of capitalistic economy, a "second nature," created by man but subjecting the masses of men to its demands and its incalculable oscillations. Since the First World War, the demonic face of this Leviathan has been unveiled. The battle against the destructive consequences of this mechanism has led to the totalitarian organization of national life, and Leviathan appears again with a third face combining features of the first and second faces. The struggle between Leviathan in its second and third phases, and the effort of individuals and groups to discover a way by which both of them may be brought into subjection, furnishes the basic structure of the present world situation. Christianity must give its message to a world in which Leviathan in its different aspects threatens all human existence to its very roots.

III: The Present World Situation as Revealed in Humanity's Cultural Life

The general character of the present world situation determines every aspect of mankind's existence. In each sphere of life, the underlying structure can be recognized as directly or indirectly controlling. In some realms, resistance against the general trend is stronger than in others, but none is independent of the determining factors.

Although social and economic forces are predominant in our present world, the spiritual realm shows the traits of the "triple-faced Leviathan" as clearly as the economic sphere, and in certain respects more significantly. The mechanism of mass production and distribution has had profound effects not only on economic and political structures but also on the innermost center of personal life, on the character of all human communities, and on the aims and methods of education.

We begin therefore with an examination of man's cultural and spiritual life, and return later to the economic and political factors which are there disclosed as more fundamental and determinative.

Changes in Personality, Illustrated from Art

Personality and community in their interdependence are the very substance and basis of all social structures.

The prophets of bourgeois society believed that victory over feudalism and authoritarianism would create both fully developed autonomous persons and true communities of those who had been emancipated to personal freedom; the principle of automatic harmony seemed to guarantee a harmonious society. But in no realm did the disintegrative influence of bourgeois society become more obvious than in that of personality and community. The "rational" individual is separated from every other individual. Society replaces community; cooperation replaces unity in a common reality.

We may take an illustration from art. The aesthetic realm always furnishes the most sensitive barometer of a spiritual climate. "Art indicates what the character of a spiritual situation is; it does this more immediately and directly than do science or philosophy. . . . Science is of greater importance in the formation of a spiritual situation, but art is the more important for its apprehension."[1]

If we study the portraits of Rembrandt, especially in his later period, we confront personalities who are like self-enclosed worlds—strong, lonely, tragic but unbroken, carrying the marks of their unique histories in every line of their faces, expressing the ideals of personality of a humanistic Protestantism. To compare these portraits with Giotto's pictures of St. Francis and his monks is to recognize the difference between two worlds. Giotto's Francis is the expression of a divine power by which man is possessed and elevated beyond

[1] Paul Tillich, *The Religious Situation* (New York: Meridian Books, 1956), p. 85.

his individual character and personal experiences. So are all other figures in Giotto's paintings. Between Giotto and Rembrandt are the portraits of Titian—individual expressions of humanity as such, representatives of the greatness, beauty, and power of man. The transcendent reality to which Giotto subjects all individuals, their actions and emotions, has disappeared; but the unique individual, as in Rembrandt, has not yet appeared. The personality which found its highest portraiture in Rembrandt's pictures is the personality of the early bourgeois spirit, still subject to absolute forces, still shaped by the Protestant conscience, but already standing by itself, independent alike of transcendent grace and of humanity. In these three painters, the development of the ideal of personality in the modern world finds classic expression.

If we take the long step to portraits painted since the middle of the nineteenth century, we are in still another world. Individuals with a highly developed intellectuality and strong will appear—the bearers of technical reason, the creators of large-scale world economy, of the great monopolies, the conquerors of the forces of nature, and the anonymous directors of the worldwide mechanism of capitalistic society. Personality has become at once the ruler and the servant of Leviathan. Willpower and technical rationality are united, and thus the way is prepared for the fascist type in which the last remnants of the classical and humanistic ideal of personality are completely lost.

In the time of Giotto, relation to transcendent reality gave meaning, center, and content to personal life. In Titian, belief in the divinity of the human and the humanity of the divine furnished the center of meaning. In Rembrandt, the experience of life with its tragedy and its ultimate hope determined personal existence. But the person of the period of the triumphant bourgeoisie was dominated by purposes without ultimate meaning and by sensations and actions without spiritual center. It was a personality which could still use the traditions of the past for aesthetic enjoyment, but which was not shaped by them. This naturalistic personality was formed by the demands of modern economy, and by neither divinity nor humanity, even if humanitarian and religious obligations were retained in the form of the moral or conventional standards of the bourgeois era.

The principle of harmony between reason and nature had promised the harmonious development of personal life if only ecclesiastical and political restrictions were removed. It was supposed that each man's personal center would organize all bodily and mental functions in meaningful unity. The ideal of personality as the actualization by each educated individual of all human possibilities displaced the ideal of participation by every man, whether educated or not, in a common spiritual reality which transcends him and yet at the same time gives him a personal center. In this fashion, the majority of human beings, since they could not share in the realization of the individualist goal, were excluded from significant participation in the ideal. They were consigned to remnants of religious tradition, or to education in technical reason and conventional morals. But even in the privileged strata of society, the situation was not greatly different. Technical intelligence replaced humanistic reason. Prophetic minds of the nineteenth century saw this transformation taking place, and they foresaw its destructive consequences. But they could not prevent it. Despite their protests, the technical depersonalization of man spread, not only in Europe and America but all over the world.

But man is fully rational only on the foundation of, and in interdependence with, nonrational factors. Therefore the predominance of technical reason evoked a reaction by the vital forces in man. They arose and made themselves manifest in both theory and practice. Whether called "instinct" or "passion" or "libido" or "interest" or "urge" or "will to power" or "élan vital" or "unconscious ground," they cannot be denied. They make it impossible to transform man into a psychological mechanism with intelligence and adjustability. They revolt against control by merely utilitarian reason. The conventional veil concealing the dynamic center of living man has been torn aside. Élan vital displaced the rational center of early humanism.

However, the vitalistic protest against the mechanization of man is as ambiguous as reactions against Leviathan in other realms. These protests have changed its face, but not its being. Consciousness, discovering the unconscious, tries to bring it into servitude to its own purposes. Instead of suppressing it, as early Victorian morals demanded, it elevates it into equality with consciousness. The "adjusted" personality becomes a more perfect instrument of an all-controlling will, surrendering itself with fanaticism to irrational and unconditioned purposes.

Changes in Structure of Communities

The development of the modern idea of personality in its main stages has had its parallels in the structure of all communities, natural communities such as the family, and historical communities such as the state.

In the first stage, represented by the pictures of Giotto, every individual participates in a communal movement created by loyalty to a transcendent reality. It is an all-embracing community in which every individual, both peasant and prince, is borne forward by the same spiritual reality. In the life of the Renaissance, outstanding individuals are predominant. They are isolated, each in his own way representing general humanity, dealing with one another in the relations of a privileged society but no longer in terms of community. The person of Protestant humanism is a member of an active group united by common purposes—the defense of pure doctrine, the struggle against absolutism, the crusade for the establishment of the Kingdom of God. This is a community, however, not on the basis of a common ground of universal authority but on the basis of common devotion to particular aims for which it is necessary to fight. The spiritual center of this community lies in the future.

In the second period of bourgeois society, not only a common spiritual ground but a common spiritual purpose were lost. In consequence, the different forms of community disintegrated. The family disintegrated into individuals, each of whom lives for himself in the service of the mechanism of society. Communities of workers were replaced by mass cooperation of a non-personal character. Patriarchal responsibility for the servant, his welfare and his loyalty, gave way to the relations of legal contract. Neighborhood as a form of community lost its meaning. The national community recovered reality only when attacked, and lost it again when danger passed. Even the community of friendship was destroyed by the universal sway of competition. Bourgeois society in its second phase destroyed community because it destroyed any common foundation and any common purpose. The service of the mechanism of mass production is not a possible spiritual center for community. It separates individuals from one another in spiritual loneliness and competition. It turns them into atoms in the service of mechanical processes. It is not based on a common idea but on the controlling economic and psychological necessity that each man subject himself to the mechanism. Thus communities disintegrate into masses. Masses have neither common ground nor common purposes. They are driven in their objective existence by the incalculable movements of the mechanism of production, subjectively by the laws of mass psychology. This was the main sociological feature of the second period of bourgeois society. Many keen observers during the nineteenth century noted the dissolution of personality into atoms and community into masses, and forecast the cultural and political self-destruction of society.

To be sure, the trends just described were never completely victorious. Pre-bourgeois groups and pre-capitalist attitudes survived. In Russia, the majority of the populace were hardly touched by the disintegration of community. In America, the Protestant humanist ideals of personality and community are still vital in large sections of the country. In Asia, the family system resisted bourgeois atomization. But all these forms are under continuous and advancing attack. The dissolution of family, of neighborhood, of personal cooperation is rapidly progressing. Even more important is the fact that every attempt to halt the general process of mechanization was finally subjected to the mechanism against which it protested. For example, European youth movements sought escape by fleeing to nature and emotional communion. But they were caught in the totalitarian movements and transformed into instruments of its authoritarian machinery. To be sure, individuals in these groups no longer felt isolated and lonely. They were organized and their every activity, thought, and emotion was planned and prescribed. Often they became not dissimilar to the "fighting orders" in the earlier opposite transition from feudalism to freedom. These groups, which now embrace the whole younger generation in fascist and Communist countries, are "commanded" communities, logically a contradiction in terms, but in practice a very effective method for overcoming the feeling of solitude which was so prevalent in the second period, much more effective than the invocation of solidarity in the labor movements of the nineteenth century. The new type of personality produced in these communities has its spiritual center completely beyond itself in the collectivity to which it belongs. The individual has become the self-dedicated instrument of a controlling will—not the unconscious and half-resisting instrument of the "second nature" in large-scale capitalism. Unconditional surrender to an unconditionally accepted purpose, resignation of any kind of autonomy, fanatical devotion are features of their existence. These are consciously dehumanized groups of human beings, very different from the automatically dehumanized industrial masses of the nineteenth century.

Thus, in the third stage of the bourgeois development, the attempt has been made to reestablish community on the basis of antibourgeois doctrines through fighting groups fired by a fanatical will to a new order of life and forged into the unity which always characterizes the fighting period of any revolutionary movement. The question is whether a real community has been born in these groups, whether a new "we-consciousness" has arisen which can overcome the atomization of a mechanized society. The situation is as ambiguous as in all other realms. On the one hand, a great effort has been made to overcome the loneliness of the individual within an absolutely devoted community. On the other hand, the method employed in this attempt represents the most radical employment of mechanization in the service of the new idea. The struggle against the dehumanization produced by the mechanism of modern capitalism has used even more fully mechanized methods and has thus carried through the process of dehumanization to its logical end.

Changes in Education

The disruption and transformation of personality and community were furthered, both consciously and unconsciously, by changes in the philosophy and methods of education.

Prior to the modern period, a principal aim of education had been the induction of persons into the living community and tradition of the church. It was significant that education originated within the church, was conducted mainly by the church, and was impregnated with the presuppositions and aims of Christian faith.

Reason as the principle of truth demands education for and through reason for everyone, and the massive achievements in educational theory and practice in Western civilization are due to this creative impulse. Humanistic education aimed to actualize humanity in each individual. World citizenship was the social goal and classical humanism the shaping tradition. Religion was recognized as one element in the development of the humanistic personality, but not its ground or center. This ideal had great power all through the first period of bourgeois society. It was set over against traditional ecclesiastical education and it produced many notable representatives of Christian humanism.

But this humanistic ideal for education could not touch the masses. It requires favorable circumstances which society provides for only a few—a large measure of economic independence, outstanding intellectual abilities, rearing within a tradition of culture, etc. Consequently, education for the masses could not follow this pattern. Either it was neglected as in England or was adapted to a more technical pattern as in Germany. In the second period, the humanistic ideal of education lost its hold and was employed more and more as a decoration necessary for social prestige or for professional advantage. Vocational education for particular purposes increasingly replaced humanistic education for a perfect humanity. In subservience to the demands of a technical reason, so-called "realistic" education based on the natural and technical sciences step-by-step supplanted education through the humanities. Meantime, technical education of the masses for the service of large-scale industry was extended and refined. "Adjustment" became more and more the principle of education, adjustment to the existing society. Everyone must receive public school education, everyone must learn those skills most useful for success in the mechanism of production, everyone must subject himself to the ideals and norms of the dominant system. For many, the main purpose of education became that degree of adjustment which prevents serious disturbance of the existing order by uncontrolled individual initiative or revolutionary group action. To be sure, this was often hidden to the educators as well as to those educated. Individual spontaneity was cultivated. Productivity was not suppressed but encouraged. Religious and humanistic traditions were appreciated and used. So it seemed to be a truly "liberal" education, faithful to the humanistic and Christian heritage. Actually, the cultural achievements of the past wove an idealistic veil over the nakedness of this education and hid the face of Leviathan who was its real master. They had lost their original significance, their power as the expression of human possibilities and ultimate realities. In the measure that education has been subjected to the mechanism of modern society, it has lost its relation to truth and justice and consequently any ultimate meaning. Thus it becomes a ready victim of various kinds of nonrational powers which seek to give it meaning.

The whole trend is clearly reflected in developments in specifically religious education. Religious education was originally introduction into the tradition, the faith, and the sacramental experience of the Christian church. This was still true of the churches of the Reformation though emphasis upon individual experience had increased. In the early stages of the modern period, autonomous reason could use religion as an element in the full development of human personality. But the more radical types of bourgeois education excluded religious education or recognized religion simply as a subject of historical interest. Within the churches, religious education either sought to adapt itself to the demands of autonomous reason or cultivated seclusion from the dominant trends in the surrounding culture. If the method of adaptation was chosen, religious education tended to become more and more a means of confirming the ideals of bourgeois society with the authority of religious tradition. If seclusion was practiced, religious education became more and more unacceptable to the younger generation. Indeed it created powerful resistance against both religious education and religion itself and thus prepared fertile soil for totalitarian education to pseudo religions.

But education without a determining center is impossible. Since the church with its beliefs and symbols was no longer the agent of educational indoctrination, the nation or local community increasingly took its place. States or cities took over responsibility for education. The nation was the community whose life must be interpreted by the teacher. Its history, constitution, and present needs were the realities to which the teacher must adapt the pupil. Many emotional elements such as language, home, landscape, friendships were tied up with it. The nation became the ideological center which demanded absolute devotion, though itself was above criticism. Here, likewise, the way was prepared for the third phase.

Vacillation in educational method between the ideals of autonomy and adjustment has been brought to an end in the third period. Adjustment as complete subjection increasingly swallowed the autonomous elements of liberal education. The breakdown of belief in reason had created intellectual insecurity and cynicism. Bourgeois conventions which, in the period of the victorious bourgeoisie, gave an impression of rational harmony had lost their power. In the totalitarian schemes, education became introduction to a fighting, and eventually ruling, group. Rational criticism is excluded. Knowledge for its own sake is discounted. Everything is related to the ultimate purpose of the group. The individual must resign all personal autonomy beyond the life of the group. Education for death, the demonic symbol created by National Socialism, expresses this final form of education in the service of Leviathan. Although there may be little danger that controlled education of this extreme type will prevail widely after the overthrow of fascism, it must be recognized that standardized communication through radio, movies, press, and fashions tends to create standardized men who are all too susceptible to propaganda for old or new totalitarian purposes.

The ambiguous character of totalitarian education is obvious. On the one hand, it leads beyond sterile adjustment to the mechanism of the industrial system. It overpasses the emptiness of such an aim. It creates enthusiasm, devotion, even fanaticism. On the other hand, it sacrifices personal life and individual creativity, the remaining elements of reason and harmony, more completely than has ever happened before.

The Christian answer to the educational problem must be given in unity with the answer to the problems of personality and community. Christianity achieves actuality in a community based upon the appearance of Ultimate Reality in a historic person, Jesus Christ. For Christian faith, this event is in a profound sense the center of history. The community which carries the spirit of Jesus Christ through the centuries is the "assembly of God," the church. But this church follows upon an agelong preparation—a general preparation in all religions and cultures throughout the world and a special preparation in an "elect people." Accordingly, we must recognize not only the manifest church but also a "latent" or "potential" church existing everywhere and at all times.

Ideally, education should be introduction into this church, the interpretation of its meaning and the communication of its power. Such education would em-

brace humanistic, scientific, and technical elements.
But it would provide meaning and cohesion for them
all. The more collectivist periods of history were right
in holding an aim for education equally valid for everyone and bearing directly or indirectly on everything.
They were wrong in limiting free development of individual and social powers by the spiritual center toward
which all education was oriented. The Christian answer
to the present educational situation must point men
toward such a community as is sufficiently concrete and
commanding to claim the hearts of individuals and
masses and yet also sufficiently transcendent and universal to embrace all human ideals and possibilities.

IV: The Present World Situation Reflected in the Economic, Political, and International Spheres

The Economic Realm

As already noted, it was the assumption of bourgeois
civilization that, in the economic realm, the welfare of
all would be best served by the unrestrained pursuit by
each individual of his own interests; the common good
would be safeguarded by the automatic functioning of
"laws of the market." This was the root principle of
laissez-faire.

As a matter of fact, there was never a time when the
economy of laissez-faire was in complete control. Since
the beginning of the present century, a trend away
from its rigorous application has been observable. State
support and regulation more and more supplemented
the operations of a free market. The necessity for such
interference has become increasingly obvious since the
First World War and especially in the days of the last
great depression. Even in America, the insufficiency of
liberal individualism for a large-scale economy under
the dominance of rapid technical progress has become
apparent. Economic crises become more frequent,
more widespread, more disastrous. Chronic unemployment with its attendant misery and despair for large
sections of the population, intolerable insecurity and
fear for others, the dehumanizing effects of life bereft

of meaning and hope for many—all these revealed the fundamental illness of the capitalist economy. At the same time, failure to maintain a sound balance between the potentialities of production and the demands of consumption, and the necessity of bolstering private enterprise to prevent total collapse argued to the same conclusion. A revolutionary situation emerged. In more critical moments when the threatened breakdown of large industries endangered the whole national economy, even the most ruthless individualists in big business sought state intervention. In these moments, they welcomed the "socialization of their losses," though in the next moment, when the immediate danger had passed, they vigorously opposed any attempt by the state to create conditions which might forestall a recurrence. The present phase of economic development is determined primarily by state interference with the self-destructive mechanisms of the capitalist economy.

But state intervention was in most cases an ambiguous device: on the one hand, it saved the monopolistic system from complete collapse; on the other hand, it produced resentment in those who were saved by it because it limited their free use of economic power.

State interference was a halfway measure which, in the long run, could not survive. In fascist countries, its contradictions were solved by an amalgamation of the leading monopolies with the state, and the dictatorial administration of both of them, though without abolition of private ownership. In Russia, private ownership of industry was completely abolished and the entire economy is dominated by a bureaucracy interested in furthering production and in the prestige and power associated with it, but not in private profits. In the United States, however, state interference has induced a growing reaction against the managing bureaucracy and a strong trend back toward industrial autonomy. In Great Britain, public opinion oscillates between the two extremes and seeks a third way in terms of an all-embracing scheme of social security with the maintenance of capitalist ownership. In the meantime, the economies of all countries have been brought into complete subservience to centralized war administrations.

The basic question in the present situation is: Shall mankind return to the monopolistic economy from which our present economic, political, and psychological disintegration has resulted? Or shall mankind go forward to a unified economy which is neither totalitarianism nor a war expedient? If the former rulers are able to effect the first course against the demands of the masses for security, a reenactment of the history of recent decades leading to a final catastrophe can be forecast. On the other hand, if the masses are powerful enough to force their way forward against the vested strength of the traditional rulers, the question will arise as to how a rational organization of world economy can be developed without the creation of a mechanism as oppressive as the "second nature" created by capitalism. In summary, how can security and a decent standard of life for all be attained according to the infinite productive power of mankind, without the complete mechanization and dehumanization of man? This is the question to which Christianity must seek to bring an answer.

Christianity cannot offer technical advice for economic planning, but that is not necessary. According to leading economists, the economic problem can no longer be regarded merely as a problem of perfecting economic techniques. The technical aspects of planning for stability and efficiency have been explored in all directions, both theoretically and practically. The problem of an economic system able to give security of permanent full employment and certainty of decent livelihood for all is much more largely in the realms of political and moral decisions. It is in the realms in which religious principles are decisive. Christianity can insist that the virtually infinite productive capacities of mankind shall be used for the advantage of everyone, instead of being restricted and wasted by the profit interests of a controlling class and the struggle for power between different groups within that class. Christianity should reveal and destroy the vicious circle of production of means as ends which in turn become means without any ultimate end. It must liberate man from bondage to an incalculable and inhuman system of production which absorbs the creative powers of his soul by ruthless competition, fear, despair, and the sense of utter meaninglessness. Christianity must denounce equally a religious utopianism which talks about abolishing the profit motive by persuasion in order to evade necessary social transformation, and a religious escapism which proclaims a transcendent security of eternal values in order to divert the masses from their present economic insecurity. At the same time Christianity must reject totalitarian solutions of the economic problem insofar as they destroy spontaneity in the relations between humanity and work and deprive the individual of basic human rights. Christianity must support plans for economic reorganization which promise to overcome the antithesis of absolutism and individualism, even if such plans imply a revolutionary transformation of the present social structure and the liquidation of large vested interests.

Politics

Politics and economics cannot be separated. They are interdependent.

Democracy was the weapon with which the fighting bourgeoisie conquered absolutism. It was, however, a limited democracy. In England up to the present century, it was limited by restrictions as to the right to vote and by an aristocratic and exclusive system of education for and election to political leadership. In France after the Revolution, it was limited by the device of a census designed to safeguard the bourgeois upper classes against participation in the control of the nation by the disinherited masses. In the United States, it was limited by the tradition of a two-party system which prevented the industrial classes from becoming an independent political power and, in the South, by a poll tax which prevents the masses from influencing policy. In imperial Germany, the power of conservative Prussia and of the king-emperor were effective checks upon the autonomy of the Reichstag. Alongside these limitations on democratic procedure, there were important outlets for the rising pressure of the masses—in America, the frontier and the inexhaustible resources of a continent; in France, the dominance of the petty bourgeoisie and an incomplete industrialization; in Germany, a rapidly rising standard of life; in Britain, the colonial empire and shrewd adjustment by the ruling classes to the needs of the hour.

Today, the situation has changed, partly through dislocation in the factors which made effective democracy possible, partly under rising pressure from the masses who have become restive under the impact of recent political and economic catastrophes and demand full participation in democratic processes. In large sections of the world, democracy has never existed. In many countries where it existed in varying degrees of strength, it has been destroyed. In still others, it has been saved by drastic modifications in original theory and practice. In all democratic countries, a marked antidemocratic trend is noticeable. There are three main expressions of this trend toward new forms of political life. In one, a single party attempts to gain totalitarian control over the entire nation, abolishing any democratic check upon its use of power—the fascist type. In the second, aristocratic and monopolistic elements seek to strengthen their control by undermining democratic methods and a democratic faith—the reactionary type. In the third, a democratically established bureaucracy achieves more and more independence and creates the tools for a planned reorganization of society; the New Deal is representative of this type. By recourse to such measures democracy seems to be saved very much as capitalism was temporarily saved by recourse to state interference.

All these varied developments prove that the theory of liberalism has as limited possibilities in politics as in economics. It can work only under comparatively favorable conditions. Democracy presupposes a natural harmony between the different interests and, therefore, the likelihood of a satisfactory balance between them. When this balance is destroyed, democracy no longer works. More particularly, democracy is successful so long as the interests of different groups are harmonious to such a degree that the minority prefers

acceptance of the majority decision to a revolutionary
effort to overthrow it. When the point is reached where
the minority no longer accepts the majority decision,
democratic procedures fail. This may happen through
the initiative of revolutionary groups from below or of
reactionary groups from above or, in the case of fascism, by an alliance of revolutionary and reactionary
elements at the middle.

The great political question which emerges in the
present situation is: Can we return to democratic institutions which have been partially abolished by the development of democracy itself? Can we turn backward
while facing the gigantic task of reconstructing a world
in ruins with millions of human beings at the limit of a
tolerable human existence? If it is not possible to go
back, must we go forward to a centralized world bureaucracy? Would that not mean the end of democratic
procedures everywhere? And would that, in turn, not
involve the exclusion of the common people from the
establishment of a world which is supposed to be their
world?

In seeking answers to these questions, a first requisite
is to recognize the ambiguity in the term "democracy."
Democracy as a constitutional procedure for the establishment of government is a political form which embraces a great variety of methods. It must be
considered as a means to an end but not as an end in
itself. It can be employed as long as it works success-
fully and no longer. *Democracy as a way of life* which
does justice to the dignity of every human being is the
basic principle of political ethics. But it may be that
democracy in the latter sense can be realized only by
a limitation or transformation of democracy in the first
sense. Jefferson's prophecy that democratic procedures
will work only as long as differences in power and property are not too great has been vindicated. New methods are demanded in order to save "the democratic
way of life" in the ethical and religious sense. Such
methods must effect a planned organization of society
which is neither fascist nor reactionary. Christianity
must support them as it must support corresponding
plans for social security and a higher standard of life.

Christianity must support both, not by technical or legal suggestions, but primarily by the creation of a new community which can find expression in political forms. Christianity must not identify itself with any particular political form, whether feudalism or bureaucratic patriarchalism or democracy. It cannot sanction democratic forms which disguise the destruction of community and personality. It cannot accept the double-faced Leviathan whether he presents himself through democratic or authoritarian structures. Christianity must declare that, in the next period of history, those political forms are right which are able to produce and maintain a community in which chronic fear of a miserable and meaningless life for the masses is abolished, and in which everyone participates creatively in the self-realization of the community, whether local, national, regional, or international.

International Relations

Thus the problem of international relations is raised. The present international situation shows one fact with unchallengeable finality: The division of the world into a large number of states, each possessed of unlimited sovereignty and right of self-determination, does not effect what was expected of it—a balance of power according to the principle of automatic harmony. The present international situation, not less than the economic and political situations, is the definitive refutation of that principle. This is true not only of continental Europe where it is most obvious but also of the Americas and Asia and the Middle East. It is true of all sections of the world, just because today "world" is a historical reality.

Balance of power was the obvious principle for relations between nations at a time when the unity of the Holy Roman Empire had disintegrated and a number of independent sovereign states had appeared. Just as in economics and politics the former bases of unity were replaced by the theory of automatic harmony, so in the world scene the religious cohesions were replaced by the assumedly automatic harmonies of sover-

eign states. There is always a measure of natural balance of power in life, but the balance-of-power theory
goes beyond this natural adjustment between all the
forces of life. Moreover, it presupposed a second principle, that of national sovereignty. Logically the two principles are contradictory; only a powerful belief in
preestablished harmony could assume their compatibil-
ity. This confidence was not wholly misplaced. As the
frontier situation in America was the most favorable
condition for liberal democracy, so the economic
world-frontier situation of early capitalism was the
most favorable condition for the balance of power. In
a world with practically infinite spaces for external development and equally infinite possibilities for internal
development, conflicts between states, though not
avoidable, were not fatal in their consequences. Always
some nations were not involved; wars between nations
did not become global wars. World was still an idea but
not yet a reality.

Today, world is a reality. The conflict between absolute national sovereignty and automatic harmony expressed through the balance of power has become
manifest. The more internal and external extension by
individual nations was blocked by world competition
and the industrial development of backward and subject peoples, the sharper and more sanguine became
international conflicts. The formation of the League of
Nations was a recognition of the breakdown of natural
harmonies in international relations. But the League,
like state interference in economics and bureaucracy in
domestic politics, was a halfway measure. It sought to
limit sovereignty, but on the basis of the recognition of
sovereignty. The League members retained final sovereign rights. Thus it saved the principle of sovereignty
as state interference saved the principles of monopolistic production. And in similar fashion, it evoked resentment in some sovereign nations guaranteed by it, just
as state interference evoked resentment in monopolist
capitalists who were maintained by it.

In comparison with the ambiguity of the League of
Nations, fascism attempted a radical solution. It wiped
out lesser sovereign states and created unity by con-

quest and economic consolidation. This destruction of
sovereignty and balance of power by military occupation may produce a trend back to absolute sovereignty.
Hate of the conquerors by the subjugated peoples is
already leading to an increase of national fanaticism
and self-reliance. It is ominous that in Asia enmity toward the white race drives in the same direction,
toward intensified nationalism and exaggerated claims
of absolute sovereignty. In the meantime, the necessity
of achieving world unity tempts the victor nations to
establish a centralized system of world domination
under their control, but raises the question whether
one group of nations can establish unity in the world
without destroying creative freedom throughout the
world. In still other quarters, there are efforts to find a
"third way" in terms of "federation."

To the latter Christianity may lend its support as it
must support the third way in economics and domestic
politics. But Christianity must raise the question: What
is the realistic basis of federation? Without a common
ground in the substance of social life, federation cannot
survive. Such a unifying basis may be found in the first
instance in the obvious economic interdependence of
all the nations. Indeed, the problem of international
relations is much more likely to be solved by this emphasis than by a direct attack upon national prejudices
and loyalties which may well be aggravated rather than
allayed by the war. But beyond the undermining of
absolute sovereignty through stressing the economic
unity of mankind, Christianity must stress the necessity
of a common spirit within each federation of nations.

V: The Present World Situation
in the Intellectual Realm

From Philosophy to Natural Sciences

In the first period of modern history, the realm of
knowledge and philosophy was the most important for
discerning the deeper character of the age. Here belief
in autonomous reason declared and justified itself to the
mind of man. Reason was conceived as the organ of

truth, in philosophy as well as in science, in the humanities as well as in psychology and sociology. The development of reason as the quest for truth was identified with the development of humanity. If every individual surrenders himself to the search for knowledge, truth will be discovered, and a "natural system" of thought and action will be established. Truth was conceived as the truth about life as a whole, embracing politics, ethics, aesthetics, religion. Although mathematics furnished a pattern of method, all realms of being and meaning were to be included in the construction of the "natural system of thought and life." The eighteenth century delighted to call itself the "philosophical century," not because it was productive of great systems but because it sought to bring every aspect of life within the sway of philosophy, in both theory and practice. Thus reason in the eighteenth century was revolutionary reason. It was not interested in describing what is merely because it is, but because it supplies materials for the reconstruction of society in conformity to what is natural and reasonable.

Very different was the outlook of the nineteenth century. The gargantuan mechanism of an industrial civilization was swelling to the height of its power and bringing every aspect of thought as well as life under its sway, thus radically transforming the guiding principles of the human mind as well as the actual conditions of human existence. Reacting against the revolutionary rationalism of the eighteenth century, the spirit of the times became skeptical, positivistic, and conservative in every respect with the single exception of technical science. The natural sciences furnished the pattern for all knowledge, and also for practical life and religion. Science itself became positivistic: reality must simply be accepted as it is; no rational criticism of it is permissible. The so-called "fact" and its adoration replaced the "meaning" and its interpretation. Statistics replaced norms. Material replaced structure. Logical possibilities replaced existential experience. The quest for truth became a method of foreseeing the future instead of creating it. Rational truth was replaced by instincts and pragmatic beliefs. And the instincts and beliefs were those of the ruling classes and their conventions. Philosophy was largely restricted to epistemology. It became the servant of technical progress, its scientific foundations and its economic control. Following the breakdown of belief in rational truth as the determining factor in life, "technical reason"—not aspiring to provide truth but merely to furnish means toward the realization of ends determined by instincts and will—became decisive throughout the world as far as the dominance of Western influences reaches.

The general trend in the first two periods of the modern development is clearly reflected in humanity's attempt to interpret itself. It is the story of humanity's estrangement from itself and its efforts to return to itself. After dividing human nature into two distinct realities after the manner of Descartes—the "thinking self" and the "extended self"—humanity detached thought from each of these realities and made each of them an object alongside other objects to be analyzed and subjected to general laws, just as one might analyze and classify a stone or an amoeba. Physical mechanisms, without spontaneity, and psychological mechanisms, without freedom, were separated from each other and then, one after the other, treated as elements in the universal mechanism of nature, in terms either of physical mechanics or of mechanistic psychology or of a metaphysical mechanism assumed to underlie both. In this fashion, the living unity of all human existence became lost in the process of self-interpretation. Humanity had become a part of the abstract mechanism created for purposes of control. It had become a part of the machine into which it had transformed the world in both theory and practice. In order to establish control of reality for mechanical ends, humanity lost itself. This self-estrangement was the price paid for modern science and economy.

To be sure, there were always reactions against the dominant tendency—old feudal and new mass revolts against the practical dehumanization of life, old idealistic and new vitalistic protests against the loss of spontaneity, of creativity, of concreteness in conceptions of man's being and of reality generally. But these reactions were suppressed as long as the bourgeois spirit was mounting in power and the contradictions of bourgeois civilization were not yet apparent. The tremendous success of natural and technical sciences doomed every theoretical protest against their universal applicability to futility.

The Aesthetic Realm

As we might expect, it was in the aesthetic realm that the same all-embracing tendencies found most sensitive and extreme manifestation. And, in accordance with a principle we noted earlier, it was in the field of the arts that the reaction from the dominance of a technical civilization and its consequences for personality first became evident.

Naturalism in literature and art accompanied the triumph of the mechanistic economy of large-scale production and its theoretical counterpart, the mechanization of all reality. Aesthetic naturalism, like scientific naturalism, started with the realm of objective reality. Realism was the depiction in word and color of a world under the domination of mechanism, the "second nature." But it revealed both the enmity between humanity and machine and the gulf between people in the prevailing society. Inevitably there was a strong reaction against realism. It threatened the society which for decades had sought to cover its brutal reality with idealistic pretensions. Thus naturalism retreated into the realm of the subjective, trying to describe the impression reality makes upon the sensual subject. Impressionism is subjective naturalism which uses objective reality with all its distortions and horrors as material for aesthetic intuition. It is a method of escape, available only to those belonging directly or indirectly to the ruling groups, into a sphere of *l'art pour l'art* in which aesthetics becomes an end in itself and man's alienation from himself is forgotten through pure aesthetic enjoyment. Thus aesthetic naturalism had a double significance. On the one hand, it was an expression of the general development of the second period, supporting its dominant trend toward a mechanized world. On the other hand, it was also a disclosure of the self-alienation in this period, and thus has contributed to the revolutionary reactions of the succeeding epoch.

Naturalism in its two forms was the great creative style of nineteenth-century art and literature. To be sure, it was not the only one. Romantic and classical opposition were always present since bourgeois society was never all-embracing. But only those aesthetic works showed creativity and progress which either were in harmony with the general trend toward a mechanized naturalism or anticipated revolutionary opposition to it. Idealism in art and philosophy was cultivated by the middle-class creators of the "second nature" as a veil over the naturalistic face of Leviathan. When the veil was torn away by the contradictions of history and the rapid proletarianization of this group, they often became principal supporters of fascism.

The development from the second to the third period is revealed in the realm of art by expressionism and surrealism. It is worthy of note that the artists and writers of the early twentieth century showed an almost prophetic sensitivity to the catastrophes soon to come. They turned away from naturalism in both its forms, either in the more mystical manner of expressionism or in the more demonic-fantastic fashion of surrealism. Expressionism has been well characterized as the warning of the earthquake which was approaching. In surrealism, the mechanisms of bourgeois society are used and cut into fragments at the same time, the real world disappears, and objectivity is transformed into a phantasmagoria constructed out of pieces and fragments of the bourgeois reality. A panic-driven humanity reveals the doom of its world in its artistic and poetic creations.

The Rise of Existentialism

Since the close of the nineteenth century, the breakdown of mechanistic naturalism in all fields of knowledge has become apparent. History, psychology, biology, physics and even mathematics entered a period of crisis with respect to their true foundations, their interrelations, and their meaning for life. A unifying truth was sought, a truth not merely theoretical but also practical. Philosophy itself helped to prepare the new situation. Against the imperious reign of technical reason yielding the detached impersonal knowledge of mechanistic naturalism, there arose the demand for knowledge concerned with life in which the very existence of the knower himself is involved. "Existential truth" was the new goal. A truth which concerns us as living, deciding men has a character quite different from the truth which reason, whether humanistic reason or technical reason, was supposed to provide. It is not general truth to be accepted by everyone on the basis of his rational nature. It cannot be gained by detached analysis and verifiable hypothesis. It is particular truth claiming validity on the basis of its adequacy to the concrete situation. Existential truth in its many forms has one common trait: it has no criterion beyond fruitfulness for life. The dismissal of reason as guide to truth is the surrender of any objective standard of truth. Consequently the only basis of decision between contradictory claims to represent concrete truth is a pragmatic test: the power of an "existential truth" to make itself universal, if need be by force. Thus political power could become the standard of possession of truth.

Truth which concerns life, it was claimed, must originate in life. But, whose life? The "philosophies of existence" are as different from each other as the experiences out of which the various philosophers of existence interpret reality. It can be the ethical existence of the anxious and lonely individual concerned about eternity, as with Kierkegaard. It can be the revolutionary existence of the disinherited proletariat concerned about its future, as with Marx. It can be the existence of the dominating aristocracy concerned about its power over life, as with Nietzsche. It can be the existence of the vital intuitionist concerned about the fullness of experience, as with Bergson. It can be the existence of the experimenting pragmatist, as with James. It can be the faithful existence of the religious activist, as with apostles of the Social Gospel. In each of these definitions of existence, truth has a dif-

ferent content; but in each of them truth is a matter of
fate and decision, not of detached observation or of
ultimate rational principles. Nevertheless, it is claimed
to be truth, possessing universal validity though not
general necessity. It is supposed to be verifiable by subsequent experience, although not in the fashion of
scientific experimentation.

The issue of existential truth has arisen and cannot be
silenced. But it is ambiguous. On the one hand, it represents a protest against the mechanism of production to
which reason as a principle of truth has been surrendered. On the other hand, through existential truth the
mechanism, the "second nature," is greatly strength-
ened. For existential truth also surrenders reason and
uses only technical rationality for its nonrational purposes. It dissolves the criterion of truth and with it the
safeguard against irrational forces.

Truth in this sense concerns human existence as such,
and not specialized knowledge, except insofar as the
latter is dependent, directly or indirectly, upon decision about the nature and meaning of human existence.
"Existential truth" need not interfere with methods of
empirical research; it does interfere with the interpretation of the meaning of such research and its results.
It does interfere with the foundations of knowledge,
with humanity's understanding of its situation in the
world.

The issue, therefore, concerns not only philosophy
but also all realms of knowledge. The steady progress
of knowledge in the special sciences is not questioned,
but their relation to other sciences, to truth as such, to
the totality of life, to the meaning of existence. It is the
issue of the right relation between empirical and existential knowledge.

In practice, it is always difficult to draw a clear line
between empirical and existential knowledge. The totalitarian systems have drawn a boundary in such fashion that everything with direct bearing upon technical
processes and therefore on the power it supplies over
nature and man is left outside of the question of existence. Technical science is not interfered with. Its task
is merely to produce tools by which "existential truths"

may be carried into reality. All other realms of life have lost their autonomy and are required to express the chosen existential truth. Thus, in the third period of modern society, technical reason is employed to execute the commands of an existential decision above which there is no rational criterion. The vitalistic interpretation with its irrationalism is radically opposed to the revolutionary interpretation with its cold use of reason for chosen ends—a basic contrast between fascism and communism. But in both cases, the idea of truth is grounded in a particular type of human existence which claims to have discovered an existential truth which is at the same time universal.

The abuses of existential thinking and the self-estranged position of reason demand an answer in which existential truth and ultimate truth are united. A very similar demand faced Christianity in its earliest period when Greek rationality, empty of all vitality and relevance for life, met a new existential truth springing from the experience and faith of the young Christian community. At this critical moment in its history, Christianity found an answer in its Logos doctrine. It pointed to a concrete event which it passionately proclaimed as both existential and universal truth for every man—the specific and concrete embodiment of the ultimate divine reason. "Jesus the Christ is the Logos." In this brief formula, early Christianity united, at least in principle, existential and rational truth.

The present world situation puts an essentially parallel problem before Christianity. It must give essentially the same answer, though in different terms and with different intellectual tools. Above all, Christianity must seek to develop the church toward an inclusive reality which unites different existential interpretations as far as they are compatible with each other and with Christian principles. The more the church succeeds in this, the more readily can it receive rational truth as an inherent part of Christian faith. If rational truth, with its contributions to the different realms of knowledge, is excluded, Christian faith necessarily becomes sectarian and exclusive. If existential truth with its practical bearing on religious and ethical activity is excluded,

Christian faith becomes relativistic and sterile. Only by a proper union of the two can the intellectual needs of our present world situation be met.

VI: Christianity in the Present World Situation

Christianity is a faith and a movement far older than bourgeois society. In its nineteen centuries of history, it has had to come to terms with the most diverse cultures and philosophies. Inevitably it has adapted itself to the development of modern civilization in its three successive phases. But the relation of Christianity to any culture can never be adequately interpreted merely in terms of adaptation. By the very nature of its message, it must seek to transcend every particular historical situation, and history demonstrates that the church has in fact succeeded always in maintaining some measure of independence. Therefore, the role of Christianity today can be seen as one of both adaptation to, and transcendence over, the present world situation.

Destructive Effects of Modern Developments

Insofar as Christianity has adjusted itself to the character of modern society, it is able to bring only a very incomplete answer to its problems, for Christianity, as it has been drawn into the destructive contradictions of the present stage of history, is itself a part of the problem. In some measure this is true of the church in every age. But it is especially important in the present period because the latter by nature has less affinity to a Christian order of life than former periods.

Indeed, in the later Middle Ages and at the Reformation, religion itself helped to prepare the soil for the growth of autonomy in all realms of life. Religion revolted against the totalitarian control exercised by the Roman church. Through the pre-Reformation and Reformation attacks upon Catholic authoritarianism, religion paved the way for the autonomous national state and the independence of science, economics, and the arts. Religion liberated personality and community from hierarchical control. Above all, religion freed itself from ecclesiastical bondage.

But in so doing, religion helped to create alongside itself a secular sphere which step-by-step invaded and mastered the religious sphere. Thus religion itself became secularized and was drawn into the conflicts and contradictions of the new society. This process can be clearly discerned in every major aspect of that society.

The growth of secular arts independent of the church not only impoverished the religious arts but secularized them. They became secular arts with a religious content instead of religious art with a universal content. We have noted this transformation in the development from Giotto through Titian and Rembrandt to the various schools of contemporary painting. Indeed from a religious perspective, expressionism may be interpreted as an attempt toward a new religious style and a new fusion of religion and art. The failure of this attempt proves that contemporary life cannot be expressed in a genuine religious style. Christianity cannot change this situation merely by ritual reforms, however useful they may be. A new unity of cult and art is necessary and this can be effected only if the present separation of the secular realm from the religious realm is overcome. Religious art pre-supposes a religious reality embodying a transcendent source and a spiritual center. The totalitarian attempts to create such a reality on a limited and immanent basis have produced only a few fragments of quasi-religious art. Their sterility in this respect proves that they lack any ultimate and universal significance. But at least they have sensed the problem, while the problem of religious art as the expression of true religious reality has not yet been widely recognized within the Christian churches.

The emergence of autonomous personalities and communities has virtually destroyed true religious personality and community.

With the supremacy of autonomous reason, the transcendent center of personal life was destroyed and personality was broken into divergent elements, the unity of which was partially maintained by the continuing hold of traditional beliefs or by conventional and technical demands. Within the religious sphere, personality fought a desperate struggle against dissolution. From Pascal's protests against the Cartesian mechanization of human existence to Kierkegaard's passionate affirmation of the "existential personality," the person in the crisis of decision about his eternal destiny, and Dostoevsky's vivid contrast between Jesus' personal confrontation with God and the Inquisitor's secular arrogance, the battle to maintain true religious personality continued. But, for the most part, theology did not follow these prophets because its effort was mainly one of negative resistance. In this attempt some present-day theology has returned to antiquated forms of orthodoxy and produced a fighting type of religious personality great in its negations but weak in its affirmations. For example, Barth sought to save Christian personality from both secular disintegration and totalitarian mechanization, but did not produce a new type of personal life. His movement did not attempt to master the new Leviathan but rather retired before it, and thus left the field to the fanatical dynamics of the totalitarian "impersonal personality."

Religious community, prepared by the lay movements of the later Middle Ages and carried to fulfillment by the Reformation and sectarianism, was another victim of the development. Religious community must be grounded upon objective beliefs and sacraments. It can be created for a short time by collective enthusiasm but it cannot endure in this form. It requires "objectivity." And, since the rise of autonomous reason, there was no universally potent objectivity except the mechanical objectivity of a technical process. Therefore religious community was largely destroyed, as was religious personality, because a determining spiritual center was lacking. There was, and still is, a religiously colored society, but there is no true religious community. The general religious background of society resists the destructive influence of naturalism as long as the background persists. But when it has exhausted itself, the way is open for new totalitarian systems. Totalitarianism, especially in its early phases,

produced fighting groups with an absolute faith, an unconditional devotion, and a dominating spiritual center. They are neither religious communities nor
religious societies, but fanatical orders with quasi-religious features in which both personality and community are swallowed up.

Especially clear and important is the situation in the
intellectual realm. The triumph of autonomous knowledge, particularly in the natural sciences, has pushed
aside religious knowledge. Either it is repudiated altogether or it is relegated to a corner, or it is transformed
by secular interpretations. The last fate is the most disastrous just because it appears to preserve the whole
body of Christian truth. In reality it alters the meaning
of all beliefs. It makes them a phase of secular knowledge, knowledge which deals only with *some* objects
within the whole of reality or with *some* subjective
processes mainly in the sphere of feeling. Religious
ideas are drawn down to the level of physical or psychological objects. God comes to be thought of as one being
alongside other beings, even though the highest. Christ
is regarded merely as a historical person whose character and very existence are at the mercy of the conclu-
sions of historical research, very much as God's
existence and nature are matters of scientific research
or of human value judgments. Faith becomes one emotion among others, or a lower level of cognitive apprehension; it conveys probability but not certainty; its
objects may exist or they may not. These transmuta-
tions bring religious knowledge into subjection to rational knowledge, and thus destroy its ultimate character.
Oscillating between a doubtful objectivity and an un-
substantiated subjectivity, religious knowledge loses its
authority. No longer does it express the presence in
every reality of the transcendent source of being and
meaning; rather it deals with particular realities, the
existence and nature of which are matters either of
argument or of irrational belief. But neither the way
of argument nor the irrational way of vindicating religious knowledge is able to shake the grip of technical
rationality, the former because it remains within the

presuppositions of technical reason, the latter because irrationalism is only a negative denial of a false rationalism and is therefore unable to create anything new. It is a well-known fact that this process of secularization has affected all of the great religions. Inasmuch as the influence of Western civilization has penetrated most sections of the world, religious faith has lost its power and the danger of a naturalistic quasi-theology threatens all nations. The absence of a Christian theology able to express an ultimate reality and spiritual center in terms of religious belief has produced skepticism and cynicism regarding all questions of ultimate concern.

Totalitarianism has sensed this situation and has formulated doctrines and symbols supposed to express an ultimate reality. It has tried to indoctrinate its followers with an "existential truth." But this ultimate is not truly ultimate because it does not transcend relative interests and concerns. It tries to invest a particular loyalty with unconditional validity. On the one hand, the totalitarian "theologies" reveal the final result of the discredit of genuine religious truth by technical rationality. On the other hand, they disclose the powerful desire to break through this situation to new ultimate beliefs and loyalties.

The fate of religious knowledge is symptomatic of the fate of the churches. The Christian church should furnish the answers thrust forth by the present situation in the economic, political, and international orders. But the churches largely lack that power because they themselves have become instruments of state, nation, and economy. After the shattering of the authoritarian control of Roman Catholicism, national churches replaced the one church. They were supported either by the state or by the dominant groups in society—the former predominantly in Europe, the latter especially in America. In both situations, the churches largely surrendered their critical freedom. They tended to become agencies of either the state or the ruling classes. Therefore they were unable to conquer the Leviathan of modern industry, or the liberal dissolution of community, or the nationalistic disruption of the world. In large measure, they became social agencies for the safeguarding of accepted moral standards. In this fashion, their influence was to support the governing classes and the existing social order, even when criticizing them within the general presuppositions of bourgeois culture. Only prophetic individuals and revolutionary groups attacked the system as such; the official churches did not follow. The latter exposed the evils of a class society; they sought to transcend the national divisions of mankind; they struggled against the disintegration of liberal individualism. But they did not recognize or understand the deeper nature of the system which they tried to improve.

Inevitably, the totalitarian attack on the system became an attack on the churches. Indeed, the totalitarian movements put themselves in the place of the church; they cannot be rightly understood apart from their semi-ecclesiastical pretensions. Since they offer an all-controlling idea, however demonic it may be, they are in fact serious competitors of the church. Their attacks on the Christian churches are thoroughly consistent. They can never tolerate a church with an absolute claim in competition with their own.

The problem for the church implicit in this situation is tremendous, especially for the Protestant churches, and most especially for liberal Protestantism. Protestant orthodoxy can hold aloof from the present world situation, at least to a considerable extent. Roman Catholicism can look forward to the moment when anti-Christian totalitarianism will be replaced by a revived Catholic totalitarianism. Liberal Protestantism can go neither way. It must, however, solve the problem of its relation to the present stage of civilization. It must not return to a position of servant to a social and cultural system whose contradictions have now become manifest. On the other hand it must not follow the totalitarian way in either its pagan or its Catholic form. Only if liberal Protestantism becomes truly "catholic" can it meet the needs of the hour.

Christian Acceptance and Transcendence of Reason

Christianity has not only adapted itself to the contemporary world in its dominant aspects. In many respects and to varying degrees, Christianity has transcended modern culture. It has attempted to preserve its authentic message despite all ecclesiastical and secular distortions. Christianity is not only a part of the contemporary world; it is also a protest against it and an effort to transform it by the power of Christian faith. This is true in both the intellectual and the practical realms, with respect to both belief and life.

First of all, it must be emphasized that Christianity has accepted the reign of reason not only as a factor in the secular world to which it must seek adjustment, but also as an agency for its own regeneration. The acceptance and employment of reason as the principle of truth have dissolved certain orthodox "stumbling blocks" which had not been touched by the Reformation but rather had been more firmly anchored by the scholastic dogmatism into which Reformation thought hardened. Thus reason has enabled Christian theology to face fresh questions and seek new answers in the light of contemporary insights and problems. Historical criticism of the Bible has liberated Christian truth from legendary, superstitious, and mythical elements in the historic tradition. The honest radicalism of this work of Christian self-criticism is something new in church history and brought values never before recognized or accepted. Without it, Christianity could not have confronted the modern mind and made its message intelligible and relevant to that mind. Much the same may be said of more recent inquiries into the psychological and sociological roots and processes of Christian thought and action.

All this, however, would not have sufficed to protect Christian truth from complete adaptation to the prevailing intellectual milieu. The Christian message itself had to be borne through the high tide of technical rationality. This has been done in three principal alternative ways which we may call the "preserving," the "mediating," and the "dialectical" types. Each type has many varieties. The first is represented by traditional theology in either strictly orthodox and fundamentalist form or in the form of moderate adaptation to the new influences, adaptation of structure but not of matter. It is due to this type of Christian interpretation that the treasures of the past have been preserved through a period when for many there was no possible way of comprehending them. The second type is represented by the so-called school of mediation from Schleiermacher, Hegel, and Ritschl through liberal theology to certain current formulations of ecumenical theology. These are distinguished from humanism by their refusal to adapt Christianity entirely to the demands of current vogues. They are distinguished from orthodoxy by their readiness to reexamine all theological issues in the light of the questions of our day. It is due to this type of Christian reinterpretation that theology has continued a living power in the church and the world. The third type is represented by Kierkegaard and his followers who, though themselves shaped by the modern world, are aware of the dangers of adaptation and mediation. The dialectical approach rejects the otherworldliness through which the first type seeks to preserve the Christian tradition. It breaks the protecting shell to reveal the relevance of its content to our time. But it does not intercept this content through the ideas of our period; thus it differs from the second type. Rather, it relates them to each other in radical criticism. In this sense, it is dialectical. It delights to declare "no" and "yes" in the same breath. It is due to this type of Christian interpretation that both the dangers of all adaptations to current thought and also the riches and profundities of tradition have again become visible within the churches. But the danger of the dialectical method has also appeared. When this type of theological thinking tried to become constructive, it simply relapsed into the mere reiteration of tradition. It became "neo-orthodoxy."

Not only in the theoretical but also in the practical realm, Christianity has used reason as an instrument of self-regeneration. Reason has completed the religious emancipation of the layman which had been begun by

the Reformation but had been halted among the orthodox Protestant churches. Following the abolition of the
priest's rule, it has broken the minister's rule. The En-
lightenment was in certain respects a Protestant lay
movement. As such it produced new ideals of personality and community. In many parts of the world it destroyed the patriarchal form of community with all its
implications for sex relations, for family, and for the
workshop. Reason has accomplished much the same
emancipation for Christian personality. It has opened it
to receive the riches of humanism. It has released the
suppressed levels of personal life. It has freed the individual from cruel religious absolutism.

However, Christianity would have been drawn
wholly within bourgeois society if it had only used and
had not also transcended reason in its practical application. Christian faith had to maintain true Christian life
over against the demonic powers of the modern world.
This, likewise, was accomplished in three alternative
ways, analogous to the three types of theological reinterpretation—the pietistic or evangelical, the ethical,
and the paradoxical types. Pietism in all its varieties has
preserved the warmth, intensity, and creative power of
personal relation to God. It has poured forth spiritual
vitality in many directions. It is due to the evangelical
tradition that elements of early Christian enthusiasm
have never been wholly absent in the churches of the
modern period. The ethical type, corresponding to the
mediating school in theology, is the most influential in
contemporary Christianity. It is not mere morals, as the
mediating theology is not mere humanism. In it personal religion and ethical concern are so joined that
religion is measured by ethical fruits and the ethical life
receives its impulse from religion. It is due to this type
of practical Christianity that the latter was able to penetrate different areas of cultural life and for a long time
guard modern society from complete relapse into nationalistic paganism. But the inadequacies of the
merely ethical form of Christian life became so obvious
that a third type arose, corresponding to the dialectical
school of theology. The paradoxical (or, in Kierkegaard's phrase, the "existential") type transcends both

the ethical and the pietistic types. It makes religion the measure of ethics, rather than the reverse, stressing the paradoxical character of all individual Christian existence, denied and affirmed by God at the same time. For the same reason, it transcends the pietistic type, which is more interested in intensity of religious experience than in the paradoxical action of God.

Through this resistance of Christianity, both theoretical and practical, against the complete domination of technical reason and technical economy over human life, the church has succeeded in maintaining an authentic spirituality and transcendence. Despite its partial secularization, the church has profoundly influenced "Christian" nations and secular culture. Its very existence was and is a signpost pointing beyond the mechanism created by man's technical skill and now turned against man's freedom and fulfillment. Through preaching, education, and action, the churches have exerted a largely subconscious effect upon both masses and individuals. This often unrecognized influence became strikingly visible in the resistance of the Christian masses to the attempts by pagan totalitarianisms to replace Christianity by tribal cults. Moreover, despite the adaptation of the churches to modern society, they have produced individuals who recognized, exposed, and attacked the system and all Christian subservience to it. The deeper meaning of the present world situation is not unknown to many individuals and groups within the churches. Indeed, against the nationalistic opposition to the religious and cultural unification of mankind, the Christian churches have created the ecumenical movement uniting Christians of all countries, Christian and non-Christian, enslaved and free. This movement is the only world unity left in the present demonic disruption of humanity.

VII: Guideposts for the Christian Answer

It is not within the province of this essay to attempt the Christian answer to the questions posed by an analysis of the present world situation. However, certain points which must guide the answer may be indicated.

1. One thing is certain: The Christian message to the contemporary world will be a true, convincing, and transforming message only insofar as it is born out of the depths of our present historical situation. No single thinker or theological movement can plumb the depths of the world situation. No merely theoretical group and no merely practical group, no one in America or Russia or China or Europe alone, can claim to comprehend the depths of the present world situation. These depths are not simply the depths of suffering or of profound insight or of proletarian revolution or of personal communion, but something of all of these, and more. The more a Christian group embraces elements from all these different aspects of the present world, the more adequately will it comprehend the true questions and formulate right answers. This means that the Christian church can speak authoritatively and effectively to our world today only as it is truly "ecumenical," that is, universal.

2. Next, the Christian answer must accept the modern development as a historic fact which cannot be evaded or reversed, and which, like every historic destiny, is ambiguous in its meaning and value. Our analysis has dealt primarily with the negative features of modern culture, its contradictions and aberrations which demand answers. The answers themselves must acknowledge and accept the positive contributions of the modern period. Here the principal point is the elevation of reason as the principle of truth above all forms of authoritarianism and obscurantism. This is a truly Christian issue even if it be fought out largely in humanistic terms. Christian faith which proclaims Christ as Logos cannot reject reason as the principle of truth and justice. The Christian answer must be framed with full recognition that the gains of the bourgeois period must not be lost from the future of humanity.

3. Furthermore, the Christian message must be illumined by the insight that the tragic self-destruction of our present world is the result not simply of the particular contradictions bred by that world but also of the contradictions which characterize human life always. History shows that, over and over again, the achieve-

ments of humanity, as though by a logic of tragedy, turn against humanity. This was true of the great creative achievements of sacramental faith as well as of the achievements of technical reason. Therefore the Christian message cannot anticipate a future situation devoid of tragedy even if the demonic forces in the present situation be conquered. The authentic Christian message is never utopian, whether through belief in progress or through faith in revolution.

4. Again, Christianity does not give its answer in terms of religious escapism. Rather it affirms that the influences of divine grace are never absent from each historical situation. It relates them directly or indirectly to the history of divine revelation and especially its central reality—Jesus Christ. It repudiates a tendency among many people, Christians and humanists, to withdraw from the struggles of our time. Christianity faces the future unafraid.

5. Last, the Christian answer must be at the same time both theoretical and practical. It will have reality only if it is the answer in action as well as in interpretation of men and women deeply involved in wrestling with the times. Despite the measure of their bondage to the present world situation, the Christian churches are the historical group through which the answer must be given.

8

The Hydrogen Bomb

The increasing and apparently unlimited power of the means of self-destruction in human hands puts us before the question of the ultimate meaning of this development.

The first point which comes to my mind is the possibility that it is the destiny of humanity to be annihilated not by a cosmic event but by the tensions in its own being and in its own history.

The reaction to this possibility—this is the second point—should be the certainty that the meaning of human history, as well as of everyone's life within it, is not dependent on the time or the way in which history comes to an end. For the meaning of history lies above history.

The third point is that everyone who is aware of the possibility of mankind's self-destruction must resist this possibility to the utmost. For life and history have an eternal dimension and are worthy to be defended against suicidal instincts, which are as real socially as individually.

The fourth point is that the resistance against the suicidal instincts of the human race must be done on all levels, on the political level through negotiations between those who in a tragic involvement force each other into the production of ever stronger means of self-destruction; on the normal level through a reduction of propaganda and an increase in obedience to the truth about oneself and the potential enemy; on the religious level through a sacred serenity and superiority over the preliminary concerns of life, and a new experience and a new expression of the ultimate concern which transcends as well as determines historical existence.

The fifth point is that the resistance against the self-destructive consequences of technical control of nature must be done in acts which unite the religious, moral, and political concern, and which are performed in imaginative wisdom and courage.

9

The Ethical Problem
of the Berlin Situation

1. Ethical problems underlie all political considerations. They become predominant when the political situation puts alternatives before the statesmen that cannot be escaped by compromises. They must anticipate them, even while negotiations aimed at compromises still are going on.

2. The ethical problem is not, as in discussions with older forms of pacifism, the right or wrong of power groups to use force. The negation of this right, I am glad to say, did not come up in the present conversations. The primitive identification between personal and social ethics was hardly noticeable. But there are social ethics, and the question of their principle must certainly be asked. It is, as I call it, creative justice: that is, a justice whose final aim is the preservation or restitution of a community of social groups—subnational, national, or supranational.

3. The means for reaching this aim must be adequate to the aim: diplomacy, negotiation, war (if necessary), a peace that does not only destroy but also makes a new community possible. War occurs when a social group feels attacked and decides to defend its power to exist and the ultimate principles for which it stands (e.g., democratic freedom in this country).

4. The decision to enter a war is justified only if it is done in the service of creative justice. Each such decision, however, is not only a political and military but also a moral risk.

5. In view of the aim of intergroup justice, a war fought with atomic weapons cannot be ethically justi-

fied, for it produces destruction without the possibility of a creative new beginning. It annihilates what it is supposed to defend.

6. In the present situation this ethical principle leads to the following political-military preferences:

Defense, political and military—not only of a nation's power to exist but also of its ultimate principles for itself and those who adhere to the same principles and are likewise threatened—is a clear ethical demand.

If such defense in particular situations is impossible with conventional weapons (as it would be in the case of Berlin and perhaps parts of Western Europe), even then this does not justify the use of atomic weapons, for they would not be means of defense but of mere destruction of both sides.

Nevertheless, atomic armament is justified because it shows the potential enemy that radical destruction would take place on his side as much as on the other side, if he attacks first with atomic weapons.

For the American strategy this means that no atomic weapon can be used before the enemy uses one, and even then not for "retaliation" but in order to induce him not to continue their use. (Practically, the very existence of atomic weapons on both sides is probably a sufficient deterrent.)

If this includes—as it very probably does—a temporary military retreat in Europe on our side (by no means a total surrender), this is a most ordinary phenomenon in most wars and can be redressed by the arrival of total Allied military power.

7. On the basis of ethical principles, this suggestion makes a sharp distinction between atomic weapons of total destruction (including tactical atomic weapons) and so-called conventional weapons, which can be directed against the enemy army and its bases. Of course, atomic weapons remain in the background, but our awareness of the social-ethical imperative must prevent us from ever using them first again.

10

Boundaries

For the high honor of this hour I can be grateful, I believe, to three border crossings made by the executive committee of the Marketing Association of the German Book Trade. They have crossed the national boundary and, as often before, awarded the Peace Prize to a citizen of another country. They have ignored the boundary between political action and spiritual work and given the Peace Prize to someone who, if he has done anything at all, has served peace—that is, the realization of a universal human community—more through intellectual work than through political deed. And they have broken through the wall, strongly fortified by both sides, between culture and religion, and as a cultural organization bestowed the Peace Prize on a theologian. This threefold border crossing is a very visible sign of the spirit in which the Peace Prize was established. My gratitude in this hour can only be an attempt to give by my words a philosophical and hence a religious and political expression to this spirit—for here, too, the boundaries are not final.

I

I would like to speak of "boundaries"—a concept which for long has awakened my philosophical as well as personal interests. *On the Boundary Line (Auf der Grenze)* was the title I gave a small book of self-characterization with which I introduced myself in America shortly after emigration. And the little book which the *Evangelisches Verlagswerk* has brought out for today's celebration is entitled *Auf der Grenze.* The American book reported on many boundaries which are universally human and at the same time matters of personal destiny: the boundaries between country and city, between feudalism and civil service, between bourgeois society and bohemianism, between church and society, between religion and culture, between theology and philosophy—and finally, on the personal side, between two continents.

Existence on the frontier, in the boundary situation, is full of tension and movement. It is in truth no standing still, but rather a crossing and return, a repetition of return and crossing, a back-and-forth—the aim of which is to create a third area beyond the bounded territories, an area where one can stand for a time without being enclosed in something tightly bounded. The boundary situation is not yet what one can call "peace"; and yet it is the portal through which every individual must pass, and through which the nations must pass, in order to achieve peace. For peace is to stand in the Comprehensive *(Übergreifenden)* which is sought in crossing and recrossing the boundaries. Only he who participates on both sides of a boundary line can serve the Comprehensive and thereby serve peace—not the one who feels secure in the voluntary calm of something tightly bounded. Peace appears where, in personal as well as in political life, an old boundary has lost its importance and thereby its power to occasion disturbance, even if it still continues as a partial boundary. Peace is not side-by-side existence without tension. It is unity within that which comprehends, where there is no lack of opposition of living forces and conflicts between the Old and the sometime New—yet in which they do not break out destructively but are held in the peace of the Comprehensive.

If crossing and reversing the boundaries is the way to peace, then the root of disturbance and of war is the anxiety for that which lies on the other side, and the will to eliminate it which arises from it.

II

When destiny leads one to the boundary of his being, it makes him personally conscious that he stands before the decision either to fall back upon that which he already is or else to transcend himself. Every person is at that point led to the boundary of his being. He perceives the Other beyond himself, and it appears to him as a possibility and awakens in him the anxiety of the potential. He sees in the mirror of the other his own limitedness and he recoils; for at the same time this limitedness was his security, and now it is threatened. The anxiety of the potential draws him back into his bounded reality and its momentary calm. But the situation into which he will return is no longer the same. His experience of the potential and his failure toward it leaves a thorn behind, which cannot be eliminated, which can only be driven out of the consciousness by suppression. And where that occurs, there arises that spiritual phenomenon which we call fanaticism. The original meaning of the word is "divinely inspired." That is what the fanatic feels. But the word itself has changed its meaning, and one could rather say, "demoniacally inspired"—that is, born out of a distraught spiritual structure and thereby destructively fulfilled. That can appear in smaller, greater, or enormous measure, in persons and in groups.

I think of young students, theologians or perhaps natural scientists, who come to the universities from the security of tightly bounded thinking and belief; who are led there to the boundary of other thinking and belief; who see their own so-being in the mirror or in the other; who experience the potential but are not mature enough for it; who fall back on the old certainties, but now affirm them fanatically with the aim of eliminating the boundaries which they cannot cross over, of bringing all spiritual possibilities into subjection to their own, of dissolving them in their own identity. The aggression of the fanatic is the result of weakness, the anxiety to cross over one's own boundary, and the incapacity to see realized in the other what one has suppressed in oneself. It happens too that, in doubt toward one's own spiritual world, one may cross the boundary, find in the new belief a new, tightly bounded security, never go back again, and develop a counteraggression: the often especially strong fanaticism of the renegade, the religious as well as the antireligious. That is the ground out of which wars of religion proceed. And if today they are no longer bloody wars, they are still battles that shatter the souls, in which the weapons of hate are used—namely, lies, distortion, exclusion, suppression—in order to eliminate the boundaries which one was too weak to cross over. Religious groups and whole churches can be driven into this posture. And it may be appropriate here to say a word about the German Protestant churches.

Perhaps before the church struggle there were groups among them which had indeed crossed the boundary, but which had not found their way back, and which exchanged the narrowness to which they went—a critically emptied Christianity—for the narrowness from which they came: a traditionally calcified Christianity. Against the radically anti-Christian attacks of Nazism the churches had to draw back on the tradition and defend their identity at the cost of narrowing the boundary of their life. But their task today is to return to the boundary, to cross over it and wrestle for the Beyond in the to-and-fro between church and culture. If the churches do not risk this crossing of the boundary of their own identity, they will be irrelevant for unnumbered persons who, essentially, belong to them. And the thorn of having failed can produce a fanatical self-approval, which tries to incorporate culture into itself and remove the boundary against it.

Another example of the call to border crossing may be given. It also begins with the individual and leads on to the situation of groups, here and now. I think of people who are confronted by the possibility of going out of their national or cultural boundaries, either for study or by personal encounters in one's own or a foreign land. For a moment the limits of their own cultural existence, their national or continental limitedness, are visible to them. But they cannot bear the sight. They cannot cross over the boundaries and seek for something Beyond. The anxiety of the potential seizes them and drives them back. And the encounter with the stranger, which is a challenge to cross the boundary, becomes the occasion of a foreign-hating fanaticism. The boundary which one is unable to cross over, one purposes to wipe out by destroying what is strange.

There is a social class among all industrial people which is admirably characterized by this conceptual framework: the lower middle class, the *petit bourgeois*, or, to use a sociologically comprehensive symbol, the Philistine. Regardless of what social class they appear in, they can be exactly characterized as those who, because of anxiety at reaching their boundary and seeing themselves in the mirror of the different, can never risk rising above the habitual, the recognized, the established. They leave unrealized the possibilities which are given to all from time to time to rise up out of themselves—whether through a person who could have drawn them out of narrowness, or through an unusual work of art which could have caused an upheaval in security based on self. But all about them are people who have gone over the boundaries which they are unable to cross. And the secret envy becomes hate.

When in the Germany of the Hitler period hate received unlimited power to fulfill itself, the boundaries were closed—so that a whole nation was unable to see beyond itself. And then the attempt was made to eliminate the boundaries by conquest or by destruction of what lay on the other side of the boundary—whether this meant other races or neighboring peoples, opposing political systems or new artistic styles, higher or lower social classes, or personalities developed through the crossing of borders. That is the demonic urge, perhaps in every person, to wipe out one's boundaries in order to be the whole thing by oneself.

Therefore, I feel that I would not fulfill my task as a theologian if I did not add a second point: first, that there are elements in all lands and also in the United States which correspond to the type of Philistine described. They raise their heads ever and again, not without success, but today in new forms and with numerous followers. And the second thing, which I affirm only with trembling, as one for whom Berlin was for years of his life not only homeland but also a religious concept: everything which I have said about crossing the boundary is true too for crossing the line which is today hardest for the Western world to cross, the boundary toward the East: It is wrong when the Western peoples are prevented by education, literature, and propaganda from crossing this boundary, which is erected not only in Berlin. We must also see what is going on in depth over there, and seek to understand it from a human standpoint—not just polemically. And I wish I were capable of saying this as well to those on the other side of the line.

The politically and spiritually responsible people of the West should fight for the point that the education of the peoples serves not only the inculcation and deepening of that which is their own, however great it may be, but that it leads out across the boundary—in knowledge, in understanding, in encounter—even if what is encountered seems to be only something standing in opposition. Encouragement to cross over from what is merely one's own—that is what can make education contribute toward the achievement of peace. And more important than anything else at this point is education in a consciousness of history, which writes historical knowledge with historical understanding and is in no sense limited to classwork in history.

III

Up to now we have spoken of crossing the boundary. But boundary is not only something to be crossed; it is also something which must be brought to fruition. Boundary is a dimension of form, and form makes everything what it is. The boundary between man and animal makes it possible to require and express things from men which can neither be required nor expected of an animal. The boundary between England and France made possible the development of two great, substantially different cultures. The boundary between religion and philosophy makes possible the freedom of philosophical thought and the passion of religious submission. Definition is *Abgrenzung,* demarcation, and without it there is no possibility of grasping or recognizing reality.

No culture was so aware of the significance of the boundary line as the Greeks. Plato and his Pythagorean predecessors attributed everything positive to the bounded, and everything negative to the unbounded. Space, even self itself, is bounded. The figures of the gods, and the temple in which they are sculptured, remain measured by the standard of the human. Limiting thought must bound the passion which drives toward the unbounded. The tragic hero, who breaks out of the essential limit, is driven back by the gods—the protectors of boundaries—and destroyed. The essential limits of life are the subject of oracles and seers, tragedians and philosophers. They want to call them back from the false, too narrow or too wide factual limits. For the essential limit and the factual limit do not coincide. The essential limit stands demanding, judging, giving goals beyond the factual limit.

In the younger generation, in the United States and outside as well, a problem has appeared in recent years which is treated again and again in literature and discussion: "the search for identity." It is the expression of a period in which many are incapable of finding the essential limit in and beyond their passing, factual limits, and not just alone as individuals, but also as members of society—national, cultural, religious. How can persons, how can peoples find their identity and thereby their true limit when they lose their final meaning in the actual limits? That is the point where the question of the boundary and the question of peace merge with each other. For the one who has found his identity and thereby the boundary of his nature does not need to lock himself in or to break out. He will bring to fruition what his nature is. Of course, in that realization all the questions of the border crossings come back, but accompanied now by a consciousness of himself and his own potential. At all times and in all places mankind has undertaken something beyond its essential nature and its limits. The communicators of these insights, upon whom religious experiences and basic revelations as well as creative cultures depend, have expressed through laws and ordinances in various ways the essential limits for all that is human. They have given voice to the conscience of the individual, the voice of his essential nature, and they have shaped the ethos of the groups for long periods. But no life process is exhausted in the law alone. Its essential nature also contains the goal, and words for boundary often also express the end toward which a life process strives—such as the Latin *finis* and Greek *telos*.

For Socrates, the consciousness of this goal was the voice of his daemon, which showed to him his essential limit in difficult decisions. In Christianity it is the consciousness of being religiously guided—or, more dynamically, being driven by the Spirit. Among peoples it is the consciousness of calling, in which the identity, and with it the essential limit, of a nation expresses itself. The world-historical results of the consciousness of calling are extraordinary. They have been vastly decisive for the manner of peace and disturbance in the world of nations. The Greeks' consciousness of calling, to represent the human against barbarism, saved Europe from the Persian invasion. Rome's consciousness of calling, to be the carrier of the idea of law, created the unity of Mediterranean culture. Israel's consciousness of calling is the foundation for the three prophetic religions of the West. The German imperial consciousness of calling created the religiopolitical unity of the Middle Ages. The Italian consciousness of calling of the Renaissance courts achieved the Renaissance of the Western world out of Roman and Christian antiquity; the French consciousness of calling, the civilization of the upper classes and the emancipation of the citizenry; the English consciousness of calling, the opening of the world in the spirit of Christian humanism; the Russian consciousness of calling before *and* after the Bolshevik revolution, hope for the salvation of the West from its individualistic corruption through a unity founded in religion or ideology. And the American consciousness of calling has created faith in a new beginning and the spirit of a crusade for its universal accomplishment. In all these cases of consciousness of calling, a people found its essential limits and sought to make them into factual limits.

But thereby occurred what is responsible for the lack of peace and the tragedy of world history. The power which is necessary for every bringing to fruition of something alive has the tendency, in the political just as in the personal dimension, to cut loose from the goal which it should serve—that is, the realization of its calling—to become independent and then to develop a reality destructive of boundaries and contrary to nature. It is not power that is evil but the power which is cut loose from its essential limit. It is most violent when the consciousness of calling has lost its creative force, and sometimes, too, when the consciousness of calling is totally lacking.

And that seems to be the case with the Germany of the nineteenth and twentieth centuries. The failure of Germany, from the middle of the nineteenth century on, lay in the fact that it developed power without putting this power at the service of a calling. What Bismarck called *Realpolitik* was power politics without a guiding consciousness of calling. And thereby Hitler could, with demoniacal ease, suggest the absurd racial consciousness of calling to broad circles of the German people—a facade, but an effective facade, for a development of power led by no true consciousness of calling.

Peace is possible where power stands in the service of a genuine consciousness of calling and where knowledge of the essential limit limits the importance of the factual limits. The fact that this foundation of politics was not admitted is the source of the German lack of peace in the twentieth century. The goal of all peaceful efforts in literature and politics should be that the foundation be again accepted. Let peace speeches be avoided which, because they cannot help, do damage, since world history is so deeply rooted in the demonic. Pacifistic legalism demands the unconditioned holding fast to boundaries as they are in fact drawn today, here and now. It forgets the dynamics of world history and the creative and correcting effect of the essential boundary.

From this there is derived a second challenge to German political education, and finally to politics itself. The first was this: to lead to a crossing of the boundary, that is, the factual limit, and to conquer anxiety toward that which lies on the other side. The second challenge is this: to lead to acceptance of one's own essential limit and in its light to judge the greater or lesser weight of factual limits. In this light, narrow political boundaries could be more appropriate for a people than broader ones. Differing boundaries could represent the parts of a human group, linguistically but not politically united, in the group's historical essence. The acceptance of narrow boundaries could be more comprehensive in advancing the essential boundary and also the way along which a people discovers and maintains its identity. That has been demonstrated repeatedly in the course of history, and today we are in a historical moment, where the realization of the essential boundaries for most lands, at least in the Western world, depends upon their devoting themselves to more comprehensive factual boundaries.

Could there be totally comprehensive boundaries? In principle, yes! For the essential limits of all human groups are contained in the essential boundaries of humanity. The identity of every single group is a manifestation of the identity of humanity and of the nature of human existence. But the situation is different today for the factual boundaries. They are marked by one of the deepest divisions in world history, between East and West in the political sense, which includes both will-to-power and consciousness of calling—a consciousness of calling, indeed, which on both sides has the character of exclusiveness and therefore, given the circumstances of contemporary technology, threatens humanity with self-destruction.

IV

This leads to the deepest and most decisive of bound-ary-line problems: all life is subject to a common bound-ary, finitude. The Latin, *finis,* means both "boundary" and "end."

The final boundary stands behind every other bound-ary and gives every other boundary the color of tran-sitoriness. We always stand on this boundary line, but no one can cross over it. There is only one stance to-ward it, namely, that of acceptance. That is true of individuals and of groups, families, races, nations. But nothing is more difficult than to accept the last impassa-ble border. Everything finite would like to extend itself into infinity. The individual wants to continue his life indefinitely, and in many Christian lands a superstition has developed inside and outside the churches which misinterprets eternal life as endless duration, and does not perceive that an infinity of the finite could be a symbol for hell. In the same way, families resist their finitude in time and in space and destroy each other in a reciprocal battle to eliminate the boundary. But most important for the possibility of peace is the acceptance of their own finitude by the nations—of their time, of their space, and of their worth.

The temptation not to accept finitude, but rather to lift oneself to the level of the Unconditioned, the Di-vine, runs through all history. Whoever falls for this seduction destroys his world and himself. Hence the condemnations of the prophets against the peoples, above all against their own people. Hence the warnings in the threnodies of the Greek choruses against the pride of the whole race. Hence the characterization which we must give to the system of political absolut-ism of our day: namely, that here are the most terrible manifestations of the demonic-destructive powers in the depths of a man. All of the Moloch-powers of the past put together do not have to show the sum total of sacrifices that have been made for them.

And again humanity stands before a devilish tempta-tion—i.e., to turn back in one historical moment the act of creation which, across millions of years, has brought man into being. There is no human group which has the right, for the sake of its boundaries, to begin something whose continuation must lead to the destruction of itself and of all other human reality. To reverse the divine act of creation is a demoniacal border crossing and a revolt against the divine foundation and God-fixed goal of our being. Resistance to the attempt to set aside all limits is something else. That is necessary because he who makes a beginning must be shown that he has not become lord over the life and death of all humanity, but is himself involved in the collapse which he has occasioned.

Nothing finite can cross the boundary from finitude to infinity. But something else is possible: the Eternal can, from its side, cross over the border to the finite. It would not be the Eternal if the finite were its limit. All religions witness to this border crossing, those of which we say that they transmit law and vocation to the peoples. These are the perfecting forces from the Unlimited, the law-establishing, the founding of all being, which make peace possible. These are they which lead out of the narrows to the crossing of the boundary. These are they which give a consciousness of calling and thereby reveal the essential boundary line amid the confusion of factual boundary lines. These are they which warn against wishing to storm the last frontier, the boundary to the Eternal. These perfecting forces are ever there. But they can only become effective if one opens himself to them. And my wish is this for the German people, from whom I come and whom I thank for this honor, that it keep itself open, recognize its essential boundary and its calling, and fulfill progressively its factual boundaries.

11

On "Peace on Earth"

It is my task to express some thoughts about the subject of this convocation and its basic document, the encyclical *Pacem in Terris*, by Pope John XXIII. I speak as a theologian who comes from both a Protestant and a humanist tradition and has tried for many decades to show their ultimate unity.

My first reaction to the encyclical is the general one that its appearance is an important event in the history of religious and political thought and may have practical consequences for historical existence. Most valuable seems to me the way in which there is emphasized throughout the document the ultimate principle of justice, the acknowledgment of the dignity of everyone as a person, from which follow human rights and obligations in the encounters of one with the other. There is no difference in this point of view among Jews, Protestants, and humanists: Jews, in whose prophetic tradition this principle has arisen and has been reformulated up to Martin Buber's description of the ego—the I-thou encounter between person and person; Protestants, who should never forget that the backbone of love is justice and that without the solid structure of justice, love becomes sentimentality; humanists, who have in Immanuel Kant's unconditional imperative to respect every person as person the highest criterion of *humanitas*. All three agree with the basic principle of the papal encyclical.

On this foundation, questions arise, some of which are rooted in other traditions and may serve as a transition to the practical work of this convocation.

My first question stems from the fact that the agreement as to the determining principle of the encyclical reaches only as far as the Western, Christian-humanist culture, but not essentially beyond it. Therefore, if we envisage "peace on earth," we must remain aware of the fact that there are large cultural groups, some of them shaped by thousands of years of different religious traditions, in which the principle of the dignity of the individual man is not ultimate. Only a prolonged mutual interpenetration, in which the West must take as well as give, can change the situation. This should restrain those who adhere to the spirit of the encyclical from attempts to force some of its consequences, e.g., particular ideas of freedom and equal rights, upon people with other principles. Such attempts are hopeless even if they lead to external victory.

The second problem concerning the encyclical refers to the question of resistance against those who violate the dignity of the individual. Such resistance unquestionably belongs to the rights of the person as well as of the group which has accepted and is willing to defend the dignity of the person and the principles following from it. But such resistance can become rebellion, and rebellion can become revolution, and revolution can become war; and history leaves no doubt that the wars over contrasting ideas of justice are the most cruel, most insistent, and most devastating ones. So it was in the religious wars when the rights of man were identical with the truth about man. So it is now in the ideological wars when the rights of man are identical with the social organization which guarantees these rights. And there is hardly a situation in which the dignity of the person is more deeply violated than in the struggles for the establishment of conditions under which this dignity shall be guaranteed.

This is true of person-to-person relationships as well as of the relation of individuals to groups and of groups to groups. There are situations in which resistance without armed violence is possible; but even then, destructive consequences are hardly avoidable, be it through psychological, through economic, or through sociological forms of compulsion. And there are situations in which nothing short of war can defend or establish the dignity of the person. Nothing is more indicative of the tragic aspect of life than the unavoidable injustice in the struggle for justice.

A third problem which must be considered to create a transition from the encyclical to the political thought of the convocation is the role of power in relation to force and the principles of justice. Power can be identified neither with force nor with authority. In several statements of the encyclical this has been done, and a direct discussion of the ambiguities of power is lacking. But without it, a realistic approach to the peace problem is impossible.

There is no effective authority without a structure of power behind it; and, under the conditions of existence, no power can become effective without coercion applied against those who try to undercut it. For power is something positive; it is a basic quality of being. It is the power to resist what tries to distort and to annihilate the structures of being. I remind the theologians of the fact that they open the majority of their prayers with words like "almighty or all-powerful God," thus consecrating power in itself. And I remind the philosophers that potentiality means "power of being." In every individual and in every group is some power of being and the affirmation of this power and the drive to defend and to increase it. In the encounters of power with power, union as well as conflict arises and the conflicts lead to the use of force for the sake of coercion. Then the great question arises: when is coercion a just expression of power, when an unjust one? We acknowledge just coercion in the enforcement of the law. Is there a just enforcement in the relation of power groups? This question has been answered for many centuries by the concept of the just war. But this concept has lost its validity through the fact that in a serious atomic conflagration there is no victor and there is no vanquished; in other words, neither a coercer nor a coerced will be left.

Only in minor conflicts does the old concept have meaning and it may lead to a kind of world police. But a conflict between those who give power and authority to such a police force could not be solved in this way. The problem is neither power nor coercion, but the use of coercion with or without justice in the necessary exercise of power.

In this connection, a fourth problem arises: the question to what degree a political group, for instance a social group with a center of power, able to act politically, can be judged in the way in which one judges human individuals. Such an analogy, if taken seriously, has dangerous consequences. It considers a contingent government as the deciding and responsible center of the group. This makes it possible that the government is asked to follow moral laws like the Ten Commandments or the Sermon on the Mount or the natural moral law for individuals—as is often demanded by a legalistic pacifism. But no government can make a total sacrifice of its nation, such as an individual can and sometimes ought to make of himself. However, nations can be expected to restrict the pursuit of their national interest, even reducing prestige, for the sake of the common good of a group of nations.

There is another consequence which the personification of a group can have. If the government is considered as the deciding center of the social body, no individual has the right to resist it. And this is the surest and most frequently used road to despotism. The group lies in another dimension of being than the individual; and the moral laws valid for the latter can be applied to the former only indirectly and with essential qualifications. A direct application of the rights and duties of the individual to the rights and duties of a group is impossible. This fact, together in unity with the three other problems we have mentioned, shows the limits of any realistic hope for "peace on earth."

This statement forces me to lead into a more universal and more basic consideration of the question of "peace on earth." We must ask: Which are the predispositions for the fulfillment of this aim in human nature and in the character of history? Most differences about the problems of peace are rooted ultimately in different interpretations of human nature and consequently of the meaning of history. At this point I must speak both as a Protestant theologian and as an existentialist philosopher. I see human nature determined by the conflict between the goodness of essential being and the ambiguity of actual being, life, under the conditions of existence. The goodness of one's essential nature gives greatness, dignity, the demand, embodied in one, to be acknowledged as a person. On the other hand, the predicament in which one finds oneself, the estrangement from true being, drives one into the opposite direction, preventing one from fulfilling in actual life what one essentially is. It makes all one's doings, and all that which is done by one, ambiguous, bad as well as good. For one's will is ambiguous, good as well as bad. And one should not appeal to "all men of good will" as the encyclical does. One should appeal to all men knowing that in the best will there is an element of bad will and that in the worst will there is an element of good will. This view of the ambiguity of humanity's nature has direct consequences for the way a peace conference should look at the chance for a future state of peace.

It should distinguish genuine hope from utopian expectations. The bearers of hope in past and present had and have to learn this, mostly the hard way. The classical book of hope, the Old Testament, is a history of broken and revived hope. Its foundation was in the first place the belief in divine acting, in the second, the confidence in man's right response to it. In both respects it was disappointed. "My ways are not your ways," says God through the prophet to the disappointed; and nothing is more often expressed in the prophets than the unreliable character of the people, who turn away from the covenant which justified this hope. Nevertheless, a genuine hope remained in Israel up to today and kept the nation alive.

There is a profound analogy between the history of the religious hope in Israel and the history of the secular hope in the Western world from the great Utopias of the Renaissance up to our day. In the movements which were striving for a state of peace and justice in modern times, hope was based partly on the belief in humanity's growing reasonableness.

Both hopes were disappointed, perhaps most profoundly in the first half of our century. We cannot close our eyes any longer to the fact that every gain produced—for example, by scientific and technical progress—implies a loss; and that every good achieved in history is accompanied by a shadow, an evil which uses the good and distorts it. And we know just through our better understanding of the personal and social life that human reason is not only determined by the natural laws of reason but also by the dark elements in one's total being which struggle against reason. In view of the two main examples for this predicament of man, the ambiguity of blessing and curse in the scientific penetration into the atomic structure of the universe, and the well-reasoned outbreak of destructive anti-rationality in Hitlerism and Stalinism, it is understandable that hopelessness has grasped large masses in the Western nations, especially in the younger generations. And it is understandable that a conference like this meets a widespread skepticism, perhaps by some in the conference itself.

But there are not only utopian expectations, there is also genuine hope in our time and in what we are trying to do—here and now—just as in those of the Old Testament. A realistic view of life and history need not lead to cynicism. But it may often ask for hope against hope, and certainly it demands the courage to risk, even if failure is more probable than success.

Where then lies the difference between utopian expectations and genuine hope? The basis for genuine hope is that there is something present of that which is hoped for, as in the seed something of the coming plant is present while utopian expectations have no ground in the present. So we must ask: which are the seeds out of which a future state of peace can develop?

The first basis for genuine hope is something negative, which, however, can have and partly has had positive effects: the atomic threat and the fear of mutual destruction. The limited peace forced upon us by the threat is in itself merely negative. But it does something which is somehow positive: it makes the conflicting groups of mankind feel that there is mankind with a common destiny. This experience of a "community of fear" is still weak and easily overwhelmed by a stronger feeling of national and ideological conflict. But it does exist as a small seed.

A second basis of genuine hope for peace is the technical union of mankind by the conquest of space. Of course, nearness can intensify hostility; and the fact that the first manifestation of the technical oneness of our world was two world wars proves this possibility. But nearness can also have the opposite effect. It can change the image of the other as strange and dangerous; it can reduce self-affirmation and effect openness for other possibilities of human existence and, particularly as in the encounter of the religions, other possibilities of genuine faith.

A third basis of genuine hope for peace is the increasing number of cross-national and cross-ideological fields of cooperation, some of them desirable, as, for example, collaboration in the sciences, some of them necessary for the future of mankind, as, for example, the problems of food, medicine, overpopulation, conservation of nature.

A fourth basis of genuine hope is the existence and effectiveness, however limited, of a legal roof for all these types of limited groups. Humanity can extend the realm of hope, which nature cannot. It can establish a legal structure which guarantees peace among those who are subject to it, not absolutely but to a certain degree; not absolutely, for everyone subjected to the legal structure can break through it for his own interest or his conviction.

Therefore, something more than the legal structure for peace is needed. One has called it "consensus." But it is not something as intellectual as this word indicates. It is communal *eros,* that kind of love which is not directed to an individual but to a group. It is said that one cannot love another nation. This may be true in relation to a national state; but it is not true with respect to the people of the other nation. One can have *eros* toward them in their uniqueness, their virtues, their contributions, in spite of their shortcomings and vices. It seems that no world community is possible without this *eros* which trespasses interest as well as law. Every expression of such *eros* is a basis of hope for peace, every rejection of it reduces the chances of peace.

And now a last word about what we as a peace conference can hope for. First of all: we can only *hope*. We cannot calculate, we cannot know. The uncertainty remains. All the seeds of hope mentioned can be destroyed before they come to fulfillment. And further: there is no hope for a final stage of history in which peace and justice rule. History is not fulfilled at its empirical end; but history is fulfilled in the great moments in which something new is created, or, as one could express it religiously, in which the Kingdom of God breaks into history conquering destructive structures of existence, one of the greatest of which is war. This means that we cannot hope for a final stage of justice and peace within history; but we can hope for partial victories over the forces of evil in a particular moment of time.

With this hope, without utopian expectations, this conference should begin its work.

12

The Right to Hope

"In hope he believed against hope."
—Romans 4:18

I

A few years ago, the humanist and Marxist philosopher Ernst Bloch became famous through a two-volume work about hope, the hopes of men in their personal lives and as members of social groups and movements. He recognized to what degree hope is a permanent force in everyone, a driving power as long as one lives. We must agree when we look both into ourselves and at human history, and we may wonder why it is so seldom that philosophers and theologians speak about it, its roots, and its justification. They don't ask what kind of force it is that creates and maintains hope, even if everything seems to contradict it. Instead, they devaluate hope by calling it wishful thinking or utopian fantasy.

But nobody can live without hope, even if it were only for the smallest things which give some satisfaction even under the worst of conditions, even in poverty, sickness, and social failure. Without hope, the tension of our life toward the future would vanish, and with it, life itself. We would end in despair, a word that originally meant "without hope," or in deadly indifference. Therefore I want to ask the question today: Do we have a right to hope? Is there justified hope for each of us, for nations and movements, for mankind and perhaps for all life, for the whole universe? Do we have a right to hope, even against hope? Even against the transitoriness of everything that is? Even against the reality of death?

Our text—"In hope he believed against hope"—refers to Abraham's faith in the divine promise that he would become the father of a large nation, although he had no son in his and his wife's old age. There is probably no book in which the struggle for hope is more drastically expressed than in the Old Testament. The people of the Old Testament tried to maintain hope for Israel within the many catastrophes of its history. And later on, they struggled as individuals for their personal hope, and finally there grew a hope in them for the rebirth of the present world and a new state of all things. This double hope, for the universe and for the single person, became the faith of the early Christians, and it is the Christian hope up to today. It is the hope of the church for "the new heaven and the new earth" and of the individual to enter this new earth and new heaven.

But these hopes, in both Testaments, have to struggle with continuous attacks of hopelessness, attacks against the faith in a meaning of life and against the hope for life's fulfillment. There are in the Old Testament outcries of despair about life. There is the despair of Job when he says, "For there is hope for a tree, if it be cut down, that it will sprout again, and that its shoots will not cease"—but as "the waters wear away the stones [and] the torrents wash away the soil of the earth, so thou [God] destroyest the hope of man" (Job 14:7, 19).

There is also a tremendous struggle about hope in the New Testament. It went on during the whole lifetime of Jesus, but it reached its height when, after his arrest, the disciples fled to Galilee. Hopelessly they said to themselves, like the two in the beautiful story of the walk to Emmaus, "We had hoped that he was the one to redeem Israel" (Luke 24:21). They had hoped, but he was crucified. In order to regain hope, they had, as is said in 1 Peter, "to be born anew to a living hope," namely, by the spiritual appearances of Jesus which many of them experienced.

Later on, the church had to fight with hopelessness, because the expectations of the Christians for the early return of the Christ remained unfulfilled, year after year. So they became impatient and felt betrayed. To such members of his congregations, Paul writes (Rom. 8:24–25), "For in this hope we were saved. Now hope that is seen is not hope. But if we hope for what we do not see, we wait for it with patience." We wait. That means we have not; but in some way we have, and this having gives us the power to wait.

The Christians learned to wait for the end. But slowly they ceased to wait. The tension of genuine waiting vanished and they were satisfied with what they had, the Christ who has founded the church and given through it hope for eternal life. The expectation for a new state of things on earth became weak, although one prayed for it in every Lord's Prayer—Thy will be done on earth as it is in heaven!

This has led to new attacks on hope, first from the side of the Jews who believe with the prophets of the Old Testament in the coming of a new eon, a new state of things in this world. They ask, How can Jesus be the Christ, the bringer of the new, if the world has remained as it was? The demonic powers which ruled the world in the time of Jesus are ruling it still today. Our own century proves this irrefutably. Not only the Jews speak like this, but millions of critics of Christianity everywhere, awakening anxious response in many Christians.

At the same time, the hope of the individual for participation in eternal life was more and more undercut by the present understanding of our world through science and philosophy. Imaginations of a heavenly place above and a hell below became symbols for the state of our inner life. The expectation of a simple continuation of life after death vanished in view of a sober acceptance of the seriousness of death and a deeper understanding by theology of the difference between eternity and endless time. In view of all this, most people today, including many Christians, have experienced the attacks of hopelessness and struggle for hope against hope. They—and "they" are also *"we"*—have learned how hard it is to preserve genuine hope. We know that one has to go ever again through the narrows of a painful and courageous "in-spite-of." For hope cannot be verified by sense experience or rational proof.

This leads to something else that makes hope so difficult. Hope is easy for every fool but hard for the wise one. Everybody can lose himself in foolish hopes, but genuine hope is something rare and great. How then can we distinguish genuine from foolish hope?

II

We often feel doubt not only about others but also about ourselves, as to whether their or our own hope is foolish or genuine. We may clearly calculate the future and think our expectations justified; but they are foolish. And we may tenaciously hope against hope and begin to feel foolish about it. But we were right in our hope. There is a difference which does not remain hidden, if we search for it. Where there is genuine hope, there that for which we hope already has some presence. In some way, the hoped for is at the same time here and not here. It is not yet fulfilled, and it may remain unfulfilled. But it is here, in the situation and in ourselves, as a power which drives those who hope into the future. There is a beginning here and now. And this beginning drives toward an end. The hope itself, if it is rooted in the reality of something already given, becomes a driving power and makes fulfillment, not certain, but possible. Where such a beginning of what is hoped for is lacking, hope is foolishness.

If, for instance, a daydreamer expects to become something which has no relation to his present state, externally or internally, he is a fool. And he remains a fool even if, by some strange accident, he gets what he has dreamed of, such as sudden success, wealth, power, beauty, love. Fairy tales know this. The beggar who becomes king is in the beggar's gown, but he is of royal blood. Those who dream without such present reality never attain their dream, even if they try, often by evil means.

But there are many things and events in which we can see a reason for genuine hope, namely, the seedlike presence of that which is hoped for. In the seed of a tree, stem and leaves are already present, and this gives us the right to sow the seed in hope for the fruit.

We have no assurance that it will develop. But our hope is genuine. There is a presence, a beginning of what is hoped for. And so it is with the child and our hope for his maturing; we hope, because maturing has already begun, but we don't know how far it will go. We hope for the fulfillment of our work, often against hope, because it is already in us as vision and driving force. We hope for a lasting love, because we feel the power of this love present. But it is hope, not certainty.

Hoping often implies waiting. "Be still before the Lord and wait patiently for him," says the psalmist (Ps. 37:7). Waiting demands patience, and patience demands stillness within one's self. This aspect of hope is most important in the hope we have within ourselves and our own maturing and fulfilling what we essentially are and therefore ought to be.

There are two kinds of waiting, the passive waiting in laziness and the receiving waiting in openness. He who waits in laziness, passively, prevents the coming of what he is waiting for. He who waits in a quiet tension, open for what he may encounter, works for its coming. Such waiting in openness and hope does what no will-power can do for our own inner development. The more seriously the great religious men took their own transformation, using their will to achieve it, the more they failed and were thrown into hopelessness about themselves. Desperately they asked, and many of us ask with them, Can we hope at all for such inner renewal? What gives us the right to such hope after all our failures? Again there is only one answer: waiting in inner stillness, with poised tension and openness toward what we can only receive. Such openness is highest activity; it is the driving force which leads us toward the growth of something new in us. And the struggle between hope and despair in our waiting is a symptom that the new has already taken hold of us.

III

Let us now, in brief consideration, turn to the hopes for nations, movements, and mankind in human history and let us ask, What gives us the right to hope for them?

A great example is the history of Israel, from the exodus out of Egypt to the present day. There are few things in world history more astonishing than the preservation of hope for Israel by Israel and the continuous fulfillment and disastrous destruction of this hope. No fool's hope can give this power; if Israel's hope had been wishful thinking, Israel would have disappeared from history like all the nations surrounding them. But they had a reality in every period, an experience in their past, a divine guidance which saved them through overwhelming dangers, bound them together as a nation through the gift of the law by the God who is not a particular God but the God of justice, whose justice shows itself when he judges his own nation and threatens to reject it, if it does not keep justice within itself.

For there was and is in Israel, as in every nation, much foolish hope: national arrogance, will to power, ignorance about other nations, hate and fear of them, the use of God and his promises for the nation's own glory. Such hopes, present also in our own nation, are foolish hopes. They do not come out of what we truly are and cannot, therefore, become reality in history, but they are illusions about our own goodness and distortions of the image of others. Out of what we truly *are*, the hope for what we may *become* must grow. Otherwise, it will be defeated and die. World history is a cemetery of broken hopes, of utopias which had no foundation in reality.

But there is also fulfillment of historical hopes, however fragmentary it may be. The democratic form of life which has become reality is a fulfillment of old ideas about the equal dignity of men before God and under the law; it could become reality because there were social groups in which the idea was already effective, so that it could grow into reality. The social principle which is powerful today is the fragmentary fulfillment of the dreams of the poor: that they may participate in the goods of life. But the dreams could become genuine hopes only when a social class appeared whose nature and destiny were one with this aspiration and which could make a successful fight for it. The belief in the original unity of all human races became a matter of

genuine hope for reunion in the moment when suppressed races arose with the will and inner power to
fight for a real reunion. In these three great events of
modern history, in the midst of one of which we live,
the presence of a beginning became the power driving
toward fulfillment.

   Is there a right to hope for mankind as a whole?
There is one idea which has grasped the imagination of
Western man, but which has already lost its power because of the horrors which have happened in our century; it is the idea of progress toward the fulfillment of
the age-old hopes of man. This is still a half-conscious,
half-unconscious belief of many people today. It is often
the only hope they have, and its breakdown is a profound shock for them. Is progress a justified hope for
man? In some respects it is, because man has received
the power to control nature almost without limits and
there is daily progress in science and in technical production. But the question is: Does this progress justify
the hope for a stage of fulfillment? Certainly. Progress
is a justified hope in all moments in which we work for
a task and hope that something better and new will
replace old goods and old evils. But whenever one evil
is conquered, another appears, using the new which is
good to support a new evil. The goal of mankind is not
progress toward a final stage of perfection; it is the
creation of what is possible for man in each particular
state of history; and it is the struggle against the forces
of evil, old ones and new ones, which arise in each
period in a different way. There will be victories as well
as defeats in these struggles. There will be progress and
regressions. But every victory, every particular progress from injustice to more justice, from suffering to
more happiness, from hostility to more peace, from
separation to more unity anywhere in mankind, is a
manifestation of the eternal in time and space. It is, in
the language of the men of the Old and the New Testaments, the coming of the Kingdom of God. For the
Kingdom of God does not come in one dramatic event
sometime in the future. It is coming here and now in
every act of love, in every manifestation of truth, in

every moment of joy, in every experience of the holy. The hope of the Kingdom of God is not the expectation of a perfect stage at the end of history, in which only a few, in comparison with the innumerable generations of men, would participate, and the unimaginable amount of misery of all past generations would not be compensated. And it might even be that those who would live in it, as "blessed animals" would long for the struggles, the victories, and the defeats of the past. No! The hope of mankind lies in the here and now, whenever the eternal appears in time and history. This hope is justified; for there is always a presence and a beginning of what is seriously hoped for.

IV

And now we ask the question of our personal participation in the eternal. Do we have a right to hope for it? The answer is, We have a right to such ultimate hope, even in view of the end of all other hopes, even in the face of death. For we experience the presence of the eternal in us and in our world here and now. We experience it in moments of silence and in hours of creativity. We experience it in the conflicts of our conscience and in the hours of peace with ourselves, we experience it in the unconditional seriousness of the moral command and in the ecstasy of love. We experience it when we discover a lasting truth and feel the need for a great sacrifice. We experience it in the beauty that life reveals as well as in its demonic darkness. We experience it in moments in which we feel, This is a holy place, a holy thing, a holy person, a holy time; it transcends the ordinary experiences; it gives more, it demands more, it points to the ultimate mystery of my existence, of all existence; it shows me that my finitude, my transitoriness, my being, surrendered to the flux of things, is only one side of my being and that man is both in and above finitude. Where this is experienced, there is awareness of the eternal, there is already, however fragmentary, participation in the eternal. This is the basis of the hope for eternal life; it is the justification of our ultimate hope. And if as Christians we point to Good Friday and Easter, we point to the most powerful example of the same experience.

The hope for participation in eternity is hope for a continuation of the present life after death. It is not hope for endless time after the time given to us. Endless time is not eternity; no finite being can seriously hope for it. But every finite being can hope for return to the eternal from which it comes. And this hope has the more assurance, the deeper and more real the present participation in eternal life is.

And a last remark: Participation in the eternal is not given to the separated individual. It is given to one in unity with all others, with humanity, with everything living, with everything that has being and is rooted in the divine ground of being. All powers of creation are in us, and we are in them. We do not hope for us alone or for those alone who share our hope; we hope also for those who had and have no hope, for those whose hopes for this life remained unfulfilled, for those who are disappointed and indifferent, for those who despair of life, and even for those who have hurt or destroyed life. Certainly, if we could only hope each for oneself, it would be a poor and foolish hope. Eternity is the ground and aim of every being, for God shall be all in all. *Amen.*